Pollarded oak in winter.

Front cover: *Aerial view of north Witham, showing the old road to Cressing as a cropmark in the centre of the arable field north of the houses, the persistent strong lines of the field boundaries, and the thin strip of ancient woodland called 'The Spring'.*

Back cover: *'Beating the Bounds' 1996. Typical landscape - arable fields, trees in the hedgerows and wide sky.*

ISBN 0 9540819 0 0

First published 2001

Published by:
Helen Pitchforth
10 Avenue Road
Witham
Essex   CM8 2DT

Printed by:
PressXpress
23 Courtauld Road
Braintree
Essex   CM7 9BD

Introduction

I have always been interested in the countryside and, having lived in Witham for many years, I thought I knew the area well. However, a series of events opened my eyes to new and different ways of looking at the landscape.

Way back in 1977, I attended a Symposium in Southend on "Landscape History and Habitat Management"[1]. Contributions were made by John Hunter on The Essex Landscape, Dr. Oliver Rackham on Woodlands and their Management, and by Colin Ranson on Historic Hedges.

This was the beginning for me of a totally new interest in the history of the countryside.

Further stimulus was provided by the New Naturalist book on Hedges[2] and the research into the relationship between the number of shrub species and the age of the hedge. Then there were two events which really sparked off my curiosity. The first was the display of the huge copy of the Tithe Map of 1839 on the occasion of the 650 year celebrations at St. Nicholas church. The second was the opportunity to study the handwritten notebook in the Essex Records Office *The Bounds of the Parish of Witham*[3] from 1815. Two fascinating glimpses of the countryside from nearly 200 years ago. I knew I had to go out and see for myself what is there today!

So when time and opportunity occurred, it seemed that a pleasant walk in the countryside could have the added purpose of examining the local landscape, in the field, in the light of these new ideas and newly acquired knowledge. Would the landscape of today bear any resemblance to the Tithe Map or the landscape as visited in May 1815? Would there be any recognisable features today?

I did not think at the time that this would lead to exploration and examination of most of the parish, nor that it would take so long, nor that it would prove so fascinating and exciting.

Recently, Warwick Rodwell[4] and Tom Williamson[5] and others have published their researches into the historic field systems and landscape patterns of this area, revealing that we live in a "relict pre-Roman" landscape with the ancient pattern of hedges still visible.

Aerial photography has revolutionised archæology in Essex and elsewhere, demonstrating continuous occupation and use of the land since prehistoric times. It has been exciting to discover support for these ideas all around Witham and to realise that the landscape we can see and explore today has been directly influenced by the way of life of our distant ancestors.

My interest has widened in the recent years. I have walked most of the parish boundary and the undeveloped parts of the parish and have found a landscape richer, more varied and attractive than I had previously known or imagined.

Oliver Rackham's description is very appropriate to Witham:

In Essex, we have the England of hamlets, medieval farms in hollows of the hills, lonely moats and great barns in the claylands, pollards and ancient trees, cavernous holloways and many fords, irregular shaped groves with thick hedges, colourful with maple, dogwood and spindle ... an intricate land of mystery and surprise.

I am well aware that there are many people who know far more about the locality than I do; people with intimate knowledge of the farms, the fields, the hedges and trees; people who could add to my survey with their greater knowledge of plants, maps and documents and local history.

Similarly, I know that archæological work is continuing and new reports are appearing and that it has not been possible to take account of them all. I know there is much still to be discovered about this truly historic landscape but I hope this will be seen an interim document, a basis for further discussion and investigation to which amendments and additions will be welcome. I have attempted to draw on the research of experts and to apply their findings to this particular vicinity and then I have added the results of my own field work.

The relevance of producing this report now is that it produces evidence for the antiquity of the ancient field system and records the state of the landscape in 2001. Unfortunately, it also reveals how much of the ancient field system and how many hedges have already been destroyed.

It is urgent and important to draw attention to the threats to this ancient countryside: threats from the pressure for development, for different farming systems, for more roads and the minerals for construction. One hopes that sounding the alarm will ensure that this irreplaceable heritage from the distant past will be valued and protected in the future.

1. *Landscape History and Habitat Management, Symposium organised by the South Essex Natural History Society. 1977*
2. *Hedges by Pollard, Hooper and Moore. new naturalist series. 1977*
3. *E.R.O. D/Du 850 The Bounds of the Parish of Witham*
4. *Rodwell: The Origins and Early Development of Witham Essex*
5. *Williamson: Parish Boundaries, Early Fields, Continuity and Discontinuity (1986)*

Acknowledgements

My principal acknowledgement is to the Essex Record Office for permission to make extensive use of the Witham Tithe Map E.R.O. D/CT 405.

I most gratefully acknowledge permission to quote from their publications from:

Alan Sutton Publishing
For Oosthuizen Susan   Cambridgeshire from the Air

Hunter J.   The Age of Cressing Field Boundaries 1997
                                     The Essex Landscape 1999
                                     Cressing Temple Environs 1993
                                     Hedgerows on a Bocking Estate 1993
                                     Settlement and Farming Patterns on the Mid-Essex
                                     Boulder Clays

Rackham Dr. Oliver   The History of the Countryside.

Rodwell   Warwick   The Origins and Early Development of Witham.
                                     Essex 1993

Winchester Angus
& Shire Publications   Discovering Parish Boundaries.

Williamson Tom   Parish Boundaries, Early Fields, Continuity and
                                     Discontinuity.
                                     Journal of Historical Geography 1986

Brain Valley
Archaeological Group For permission to use their aerial photographs

Thanks

For their careful work in preparing the maps, I am indebted to my daughter Peggy Morris and Valerie Carpenter. My brother-in-law Henry Ruff has prepared the block diagrams, and given much patient advice with the text and John Lambert provided great assistance with the editing. Janet Gyford gave me help and encouragement to start this project and then again to finish it! When the word processor threatened my composure, I have been immensely grateful to Maureen and Michael Scollan for their unfailing support.

Tom Henderson has generously provided sources of information and shared his wide knowledge with me and added much needed clarity to my ideas and writing.

However, any mistakes or wrong interpretations are mine.

Finally, I would like to dedicate this publication to the late Mrs.Liza Kennedy, who not only encouraged me in the project, but cheerfully walked and recorded the hedges with me.

H.P. May 2001

Summary

This is a report on the Witham country-side today, its origins and history, its content and condition. But it is also a plea for awareness of this ancient, varied, rich and pleasant landscape. It is our heritage. It can so easily be lost for ever.

The Parish of Witham has been studied and the present day landscape compared with the Tithe Map of 1839-43[1]. Research documents, maps and publications by Dr. Oliver Rackham, Warwick Rodwell and Tom Williamson are quoted giving evidence for the continuity of agriculture and field systems in the Witham area from the Iron Age to the present day.

The landscape features they describe, including the river crossings and network of roads, have been examined. Evidence is presented to show how the character of the present landscape is directly related to the pre-Roman systems of agriculture, land holding, settlement patterns and social structure.

Hooper's method of counting the shrub species was used to estimate the age of the hedges. Out of over 200 sampled, 65% contained 4 or more species and are probably at least 400 years old. Hedges rich in species, particularly those regarded as indicators of old hedges, were found to be widespread.

The topography, and the natural or semi-natural features of the parish boundary are described.

The *Perambulation of the Parish Boundary*[2] has provided an amazing link with the people of Witham nearly 200 years ago. The boundary is just about recognisable and probably 5 or 6 of the pollards bearing 'marks' in 1815 are still with us.

Major changes in the landscape since 1839, such as the railways and the by-pass are listed and mapped.

The woodlands are listed and the three surviving woods described. The map shows existing, previous, and more recently planted woodland.

An estimate has been made of the rate and extent of loss of hedgerows. About 70% of the hedges on the Tithe Map have gone, 30% due to changing farming practices and about 40% due to development.

There are also sections on field names and hedgerow trees.

This report is an attempt to take a comprehensive view of the whole parish, and the history, features, and characteristics of the landscape.

1. Witham Tithe Map 1839 - 43. Ref. E/R.O. D/C. T. 405
2. The Bounds of the Parish of Witham E.R.O. D/Du 850

Contents

Footnotes referred to in the text are to be found at the end of each chapter

List of Maps

List of Illustrations

1 Beating the Bounds

Our ancestors who first marked out the Parish Boundaries 1000 years ago, were probably unable to read or write and as there were no maps for reference, the boundaries had to be recognisable and memorable. Where existing natural lines such as streams could not be followed, the marks were put on the most permanent features such as boulders, but in stoneless Essex, trees were used.

Witham is most fortunate in having in the Essex Record Office, the 1815 account of the age old ritual of *Beating The Bounds*[1]. This notebook, hand written in 1815, (just a few weeks before the battle of Waterloo) gives great detail of what the group of local worthies and youngsters found on their inspection. They went down hedges, across stiles, through gates and from one marked tree to another. The countryside as described nearly 200 years ago, was a pattern of hedges and trees which is just about recognisable today, in spite of the loss of many hedges, most of the gates, and the almost total demise of the hedgerow elms.

As soon as I read this account, I knew I wanted to "Beat the Bounds" for myself to see how much had changed after nearly 200 years. I thought the direct link provided by this little book was a good starting point for the whole project.

Beating The Bounds, traditionally carried out during Rogationtide at the end of May, was an inspection of the boundary to see if the *marks* were visible or needed replacing. But more than that, it was a way of impressing on the younger generation, the importance of knowing the line of the boundary. It was also an occasion for blessing the crops.

Beating of The Bounds in 1815 took place over two days.

On Thursday, May 11th, a party of 22 people, landowners, farmers and mill owners and including 3 ladies and 9 juniors, met at *The Round Post on the right hand side of the great road leading to Chelmsford* (by Lynfield Garage). They went *Right Hand Round* i.e. northwards, across fields with evocative names like Weather Walls, Wood Field, Annikers and Great Breech. This brought them past Wood End Farm to a wooded area. On the Witham side they would have seen the 9 acre Lower Grove (which has now gone) and on the Hatfield Peverel side a small wood called Job's Spring. The railway here is in a deep cutting and part of Job's Spring was removed in the process, but there is a rich mixture of trees and shrubs remaining including one of the two areas of hornbeam trees in the parish.

A little way further north from the railway is Warborough which exists only as a crop mark indicating a substantial Iron Age enclosure, from where there is a distant view of St. Nicholas Church standing prominently on Chipping Hill.

I do not know who Peg Millar was, but the lane which forms the boundary with Terling is a good example of an ancient route, sinuous, with a pronounced kink in one place. Near the junction with the Terling Road, named the Four Releet, the group would have seen some of the most varied hedges in the parish in all the freshness of Springtime.

About half a mile north of this junction there is a large impressive pollard oak on the verge which could well be the same as mentioned as a *mark* in 1839. It is certainly a splendid tree and as near as possible to the furthest corner of the parish.

At the further corner of Gibbon's Ground, they turned right over a water stile by a pollard oak, and they followed the undefined boundary across former woodland and along the Great Waterfall in to the Hop Ground and to Little Tutty near Powers Hall.

On reaching the Notley Road they turned left and *after about 36 rods turned right into Major Bullock's Warren Field, leading into Major Bullock's Dick Mead where Mr. Thomas Barnes Junior was bumped against a tree.* Presumably the bumping was sufficiently hard to assist the memory, and not too hard to curtail the rest of the inspection!

It is not clear why sometimes there is great detail as to ownership of the fields, as with Major Bullock's fields, yet other fields are not mentioned at all.

Then there seems to have been some confusion near the river:

Then you go from the fourth tree on the second road which is a timber elm marked but we did not mark this elm not knowing whether it was in the hedge of Whitebridge Field where this row of trees has been thrown down and the fields passed into the parks since May 26th 1783.

(What happened on that very precise date? Does this refer to emparkment by Faulkbourne Hall?)

Then there was an incident. *On the corner of Whitebridge Field was a trap baited with a rat and set near the river by the game keeper for the purpose of taking carrion crow. One had pounced upon the trap and caught by the legs. It was taken out by Mr. Thomas Barnes Junior, killed and thrown into the river.* (The bumping cannot have hurt him too much!)

Once across the river, it was straight along what was then the road from Witham to Cressing. It is now a grassy sunken track, with the remnants of hedges and banks and a few tall trees. They went *to a seat near Hungary Hall* where they *had bread and cheese and beer brought by Mr. Joseph Beadle Senior from two public houses in Chipping Hill.*

After lunch, the walkers went round Ozhod, the field opposite Hungary Hall, now divided by the Braintree railway, and described in great detail. Then across Church Field (the most distant part of the land belonging to the Vicarage), past Whiteheads Farm, through Vicarage Wood, (still a wood then) to the green lane, sometimes called Oliver's Lane. The lane obviously pre-dates the boundary and was a well established feature, yet it is followed for only two fields.

The boundary walkers continued to cross fields, checking on banks and hedges, and marked trees until they reached Rickstones Road, near the site of the present school. They passed Little Elms Farm which is now Little Elms Pub, and Half Hides Farm, followed Cut Throat Lane and Motts Lane to the High Road.

But they still had not finished, for they had to turn left to inspect the detached section of the parish consisting of the four fields, Great, Little and Upper Goswells, (Goslings) and Burgy Field, then at last they were able to *go over by the hedge to the Great Road which is the finish of the first day.*

On the second day, Friday May 12th, 26 people including 3 undaunted ladies and 7 juniors from the previous day, continued the inspection. They met near Lynfield, but this time at the *hand post on the left hand side of the road leading into Chelmsford.* The first part of the boundary winds its way round the small fields of Latneys, before going off southeast to another Grove Wood. The wood was grubbed about 70 years ago, and although the boundary has been obliterated by the line of the new A12, there is a remnant of a species-rich hedge.

South from Dengie Farm the boundary has a strange double kink in it, while other field boundaries are unusually straight, features which probably reflect some hidden aspect of their history In one of them called Cloddy Pieces, James Catchpool was *bumped.*

They followed the line to where it crosses Maldon Road near a modern bungalow and then across to the River Blackwater through Olivers Farm. Strangely, there is no mention as to how they crossed the river. Tantalisingly, the account merely says *continue across the river called Goodwins Deep to an alder marked and go straight across Sparkey Mead.*

From the river, the boundary crosses the new golf course, up to an excellent viewpoint near an Iron Age settlement above Blue Mills, before emerging on to the road at the junction with Mope Lane. From there the party continued *up the middle of the road to Four Crossways* and then the cheerful statement: *We went to The Chequers and lunched.*

After lunch, the walkers went in and out of fields and woods in an area where the boundary is not easy to follow. Then, as a note explains, *they took the whole of Chantrey Wood into Witham parish.* This must have been for convenience, because Chantrey Wood was divided between two parishes.

From there down to the River Blackwater, they went from tree to hedge to tree, making it difficult to follow on the map. Again, there is no clue as to how they crossed

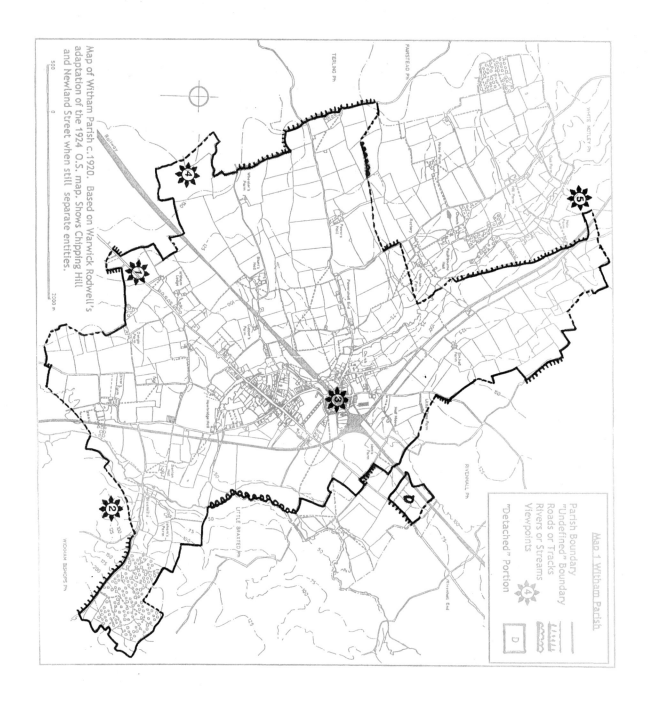

Map of Witham Parish c.1920. Based on Warwick Rodwell's adaptation of the 1924 O.S. map. Shows Chipping Hill and Newland Street when still separate entities.

Map 1 Witham Parish

Parish Boundary
"Undefined" Boundary
Roads or Tracks
Rivers or Streams
Viewpoints
"Detached" Portion

the River Blackwater, just *cross directly over into Mr. Jossleyn's Whet Mead.* They followed the northern bank through Whetmead, now a Local Nature Reserve, and Sharp Mead into Broad Mead. This meadow was divided into narrow strips to give the different owners a share of the valuable hay crop. An indication of the value was that half the strips were still in 1839 owned by Cressing Temple, which is about three miles away. From Broad Mead, it was a short step to Braxted Lane and into the great road from Colchester.

On the final page of the notebook is the summary:

Met the first day at Latneys at half past nine in the morning and finished at Burgy Brook at a quarter past seven in the evening. Dined at the White Hart at a quarter before eight.

Met the second day at ten o'clock in the morning and finished at the lane leading to Little Braxted at half past four. Dined at the Spread Eagle at a quarter past five.

The young lads dined both days with Mr. Barnes and the rest of the gentlemen. (Where were the ladies?!) *Each of the youngsters had a glass of wine given and retired.*

I should think they all had good appetites after nearly ten hours on the first day and over 6 on the second! It is good to know that the pubs they patronised in 1815, The Chequers, The Spread Eagle, and The White Hart are still in existence and under the same names and still ready, no doubt, to serve anyone who "Beats The Bounds" in the year 2001.

In 1815, there were 92 *marks* in the nearly 20 miles of boundary, 84 of them were on trees and only three on posts.

The trees named are:

Elm	34 including 27 pollards
Oak	36 including 15 pollards
	8 including 2 pollards
Maple	11 including 1 pollard
Hornbeam	2 and 2 alder

A pollard is a tree which has been cut at 8'-12' above ground and allowed to grow again. Pollards are generally more noticeable and often much older than timber trees, adding considerably to the interest and character of the landscape with their gnarled trunks and strange shapes.

I found the proportions of tree species to be about the same today, with the great exception of elm which has almost disappeared as a hedgerow tree.

It is a direct indication of the differences between farming in 1815 and the present day, that most of the gates and stiles have disappeared. Then, there would have been grazing animals on each farm, and strays could get lost or damaged and cause accidents or damage crops. Now the farms are almost entirely arable and the gateways have been widened to accommodate large farm machinery.

The 1815 account gives a vivid picture of the countryside of nearly 200 years ago. With some difficulty, mainly due to the lack of punctuation marks in the original document, I have been able to place the *marks* on a large scale map. This exercise has revealed, amongst other things, that 6 pollards, alive and well in the year 2001, are probably those mentioned in 1815. There is real pleasure and excitement at seeing and touching such living links with the past.

One particular puzzle remains. On the O.S. Map of 1874, 3 stones are mentioned, all sited along Peg Millars Lane on the boundary with Terling. I have not found any trace of them. Perhaps someone can shed some light on the subject?

It would be interesting to know for how long the custom of "Beating the Bounds" was maintained after 1815, and whether there are any records of such occasions. There is something of a revival of interest recently in such customs. On such an event there is a delightful sense of exploring the countryside, and of following literally in the footsteps of previous generations.

On two occasions recently, I have organised walks to Beat the Bounds along the more accessible stretches of the boundary. Most of the Parish Boundary is not on public footpaths so permisson was obtained from the landowners to cross their land.

On one day we completed most of the northern section, and were impressed by the stamina required! Each of the modern "perambulations" was at the traditional time of Rogation-Tide in May when the crops are well established, and one can begin to anticipate harvest, and enjoy the countryside, alive with bluebells, larksong and cowslips. Even with today's depleted wildlife we experienced all of these, and hoped that in another 200 years our successors would be as fortunate!

1. *The Bounds of the Parish of Witham E.R.O. D/Du 850*

2   The Land and the Landscape

The landscape of Essex is often, but mistakenly, regarded as flat and lacking in interest. There may be no high hills or steep inclines, nor wide flowing rivers, but neither is it flat. It is more accurately described as surprisingly varied and gently rolling.

Geologically, Witham Parish is a complex area with three main zones:

• the Wickham Bishops ridge,

• the valley of the River Blackwater,

• and the gently rising plateau to the north.

Here I must point out that I am writing about the parish as it was at the time of the Tithe Map in 1839, and as it had probably existed since about 800 A.D. So the area to the east of the River Blackwater which was transferred to Maldon District in 1985 has been included, but not the post war extension of housing beyond Forest Road.

The Wickham Bishops ridge is generally over 200' high and consists of London Clay with patches of sand and gravel. The London Clay which underlies most of Essex and may be up to 200-300' thick, was formed in shallow seas millions of years ago and consists of fine particles, making it heavy and difficult to drain or work. The Witham section is woodland today and has probably been so since the last Ice Age. The highest point in the parish is 242' at Wickham Bishops crossroads and from here the road descends quite steeply to 46' at Blue Mills, almost the lowest point.

Blue Mills is situated in the broad valley of the Blackwater, which is largely made up of deep deposits of sand and gravel, washed out of the glaciers by melting water over a long period of time, and sorted and transported by water. The deposits cover the London Clay by up to 30'. These gravels can produce good crops with the benefit of irrigation. However, much of this land has been substantially covered with post-war development.

The land to the east of the Brain Valley and north of the Blackwater valley rises gently towards Cressing, 165' at Hungry Hall. This is the landscape of the Chalky Boulder Clay, or Till, the huge deposits left by the last glaciation about 10,000 years ago, which is very recent in geological terms. The glacier in its southward progress across the land, collected and ground up a mixture of chalk, shales, clays, flints and boulders, which was deposited when the glacier melted. The Till is up to 35' deep in this area, remarkably uniform at depth, but more varied at the surface. The plateau it forms is cut through by the River Brain in a relatively steep valley, exposing London Clay and gravels on the valley sides.

The important difference between the Till and London Clay is the chalk content of the Till, which makes it more workable and more fertile. The clay component in the mixture ensures that even in this area of low rainfall, the moisture retention is sufficient to sustain arable crops. So long as drainage is maintained, the Till is very productive and can be cropped for many years without the structure deteriorating.

In White's Directory for 1848, the Till is described as "a sound turnip loam".

There are two other deposits to mention: Brickearth and Head. Brickearth was formed when the meltwaters from the glaciers slowed down, formed ponds or lakes and deposited the finer particles. It is good quality land and can be used for arable crops or fruit growing. Head, found on the valley sides, is even more of a mixture than the Chalky Boulder Clay. It may contain sandy clay, clayey gravel, gravel, flint and chalk. These unrelated materials, only partially weathered, were assembled by the movement of waters during the periods of alternate permafrost and seasonal thaw. Both the Brickearth and Head are largely built over now.

Viewpoints

In order to have an overall view, and to have a good look at the gently rolling and surprisingly varied countryside of the parish of Witham, it is worth visiting 5 viewpoints. (See Map 1)

The first is on the bridge over the A12 near Lynfield Garage, very near the Iron Age settlement at Witham Lodge. From here at a height of nearly 150' one can look west across the wide valley, sloping down to Blue Mills at 46' and up to the Wickham Bishops ridge and the highest point in the parish, 242'. Virtually all the land one can see to the east of the bypass is designated in the Braintree District Local Plan as either Green Wedge or of Special Landscape Value, official designations which should help protect this scenically important area from development.

A view does not end at a parish boundary and so it is good to know that the land formerly in Witham (east of the River Blackwater) which is now in Maldon District Council, has similar protection.

The second viewpoint is at a height of 100' where the footpath leading from Blue Mills across the golf course approaches the edge of the Iron Age settlement of Mope Wood. This is a surprisingly good viewing point, overlooking in a wide sweep, several miles of the Blackwater valley, north towards Kelvedon, west across towards Hatfield Peverel, and including the built-up part of Witham.

The third vantage point is also at about 100', from the height of the Iron Age fortifications at Chipping Hill. As a view point now, Chipping Hill is somewhat limited by the spread of development, but formerly one could see a long way south and west, up and down the Brain valley. This relatively high spot has been the focal point for tracks and roads since pre-historic days. The church tower is still a surprisingly prominent landmark on approaching Witham from all directions, except the main road in from Colchester, where it is obscured by the huge grain silos near the station.

The fourth vantage point, one that is very important historically, is the Iron Age site of Warborough, which at 157' is the highest point on the Chalky Boulder Clay plateau between Witham and Terling. The height may not be very great, but from Warborough there is a sense of space, and the eye is led across the fields right back to the church tower at Chipping Hill and the houses surrounding it.

The fifth viewpoint is from the furthest corner of the field with the strange name of Ozhod. Perhaps its strange situation as an inexplicable extension of the parish, the only field to the west of the road from Witham towards Cressing, is connected to the fact that four parishes meet here. From the western end of Ozhod one can overlook a long section of the Brain valley both north and south, at a point where it is beginning to narrow.

It cannot be just coincidence that the best views are obtained from sites associated with the pre-Roman inhabitants, and their settlements, even though they were probably more interested in keeping watch from vantage points than in admiring the view!

3   The Origins of the Parish System and the Development of Witham Parish

During the period 650 to 1000 A.D. the worship of heathen gods in England was gradually Christianised and churches were built. One of the earliest in England following the successful mission of St. Cedd to this county in 653 A.D. was St. Peter's at Bradwell on Sea, about 20 miles from Witham on the Essex coast.

Many of the earliest churches were "Minster" churches, often of royal foundation, established in the 7th or 8th centuries, serving a wide area as centres for pastoral care, administered by the bishops and with any tithe being paid to the bishops. Rodwell[1] suggests that Witham was probably a "Minster" church, covering the same large area as a royal manor.

The early church in England was part of the wider church in Europe, so when Charlemagne who reigned from 768 to 814 A.D. created church law, it applied to England. He deemed that pastoral work should be carried out by a single priest, in a parish of one village, or a small group of adjacent villages. Payment of tithes, previously voluntary, became obligatory and the income thus raised, made possible the building of churches. Every person had to pay a tenth of their produce or profit to the church. The parish came to consist of the land from which the tithes were paid to a particular church, thereby creating the need for recognisable parochial boundaries.

It is an interesting reflection on the importance attached to the provision of opportunities for worship and instruction for every Christian, that there was spectacular growth in the number built in the 10th and 11th centuries. There were so many, that, by and large, they were sufficient until the great growth in population at the time of the Industrial Revolution. By 1200 A.D. there were 410 churches in Essex, 102 of them built with substantial re-cycling of Roman material.

Parish churches were mostly founded by lay landowners, keen to provide for the need for Christian worship. They came to be endowed with the tithes from the founder's estate and the parochial boundaries became established out of the earlier and probably vaguer territory of the minster church.

By the reign of Ethelred the Unready, 978-1016 A.D., each diocese was being organised on the basis of a pastoral system based on parish units, each with a church with its priest and endowment. The landowner who founded the church, had certain rights in the appointment of the priest and administration of the endowment, but the bishop defined the area of the parish and only the bishop could approve or remove the priest. The priest's duty was to conduct divine office and the mass, to provide instruction for parishioners, to visit the sick and the poor, and to attend to the needs of strangers. For these services, he was provided with an income. The tithes were divided into 4 parts: one for the bishop and the diocese: one for the upkeep of the church: one to provide for the poor and travellers, and one for the priest. There was also the income from the Glebe land, which in the east of England was usually between 15 and 30 acres. The two sources of income together provided the endowment of the church.

It is not known exactly when Parish Boundaries were set out, but Angus Winchester[2] tells us that once the payment of tithes to the church was made obligatory, it would have been a matter of great importance to the parishioners and the clergy as to which parish received the tithe. At some time in the centuries before the Norman Conquest, representatives of Witham landowners and the parish and its 11 neighbouring parishes, must have met and discussed and decided where each boundary would be. It is likely that for convenience, the boundaries of existing estates or manors would have been adopted for those of the parish.

Those early boundary commissioners were members of long established farming communities to whom the ownership of land and its quality were most important matters. This was nothing new. Boundaries would have been hard won with all the physical labour of clearing woodland and for that reason were not lightly altered. A field might change owners, but was less likely to change its shape or boundaries. Landlords and ruling classes come and go, but farming, the provision of food, goes on.

When parishes were being established, consideration had to be given to the viability of each parish as a community in order to support their way of life. Each settlement would need access to the staples of life:

- arable land for food crops, wheat, barley and beans
- water meadows for the all important hay crops
- "Moors" or rough grazing for animals throughout the year
- woodland for fuel, building materials and food e.g. acorns for pigs
- possibly access to river transport and boats may have been a consideration, for heavy or imported goods, as perhaps with the detached portions of Faulkbourne parish at the eastern end of Witham.)

When considering church organisation in Witham, Rodwell presents evidence for the early creation of a "Minster" church. This would have served a wider area than a parish and in some instances would have been linked to a royal estate.

Rodwell: *There can be little doubt that Witham minster was a royal foundation endowed with a sizeable block of land stretching from Rivenhall Wood to the meadows of the Brain valley. The provision of Glebe for Rivenhall and Faulkbourne would have become necessary on their establishment as independent units. This is most likely to have been before 1185.*

The 1839 Tithe Survey reveals a complicated situation of Glebe lands and detached portions of Witham, Faulkbourne and Rivenhall. This seems to imply the existence of a previous estate which was large enough for Rivenhall and Faulkbourne to be separated off and also to provide Glebe land and detached portions for each parish. The detached portion of Faulkbourne retained access to the River Blackwater, Little Braxted Mill and the valuable hay meadows by the river.

By way of contrast, when King Stephen granted land to the Knights Templar in 1147, it was a large block of land including the fields between the north of Witham and Cressing Temple Farm. This act completed the break-up of the Minster estate.

The division of the Minster estate into separate parishes was not the only major change. Essex was subjected to successive invasions by the Anglo-Saxons and the Danes. The Anglo-Saxons seem to have settled near the coast in Essex and the Danes were sufficiently in control of the rest of the county for it to have been part of the "Danelaw".This was the area of pre-Norman England, from the River Tyne to the River Thames, east of Watling Street, within which Danish laws and customs prevailed from the late 9th to the late 11th centuries.

The Danes are thought to have arrived in smaller numbers than the Anglo-Saxons. Therefore, there was less need to evict the original inhabitants in order to obtain farmland for themselves. They took control of the social and civic systems but did not change the agricultural systems.

Where the influence of the Anglo-Saxons was decisive it was usual for the Open Three Field System to become established. In order for this system to be viable, considerable relocation of people into villages was necessary.

There is no evidence for this major change in farming methods and social re-organisation in the Witham area. Perhaps the style of agriculture, or the independence of the settlers/farmers, or even of the local inhabitants, did not lend itself to the more co-operative type of farming necessary in the Open Field System.

There no evidence at all that the Witham pre-historic system of enclosure was ever altered to provide Open Fields, neither is there any evidence for subsequent re-enclosure. Therefore, this provides further support for the pre-historic origin and survival of the local landscape.

It is worth repeating W. G. Hoskins'[3] dictum, that boundaries, whether of parish, estate, hundred or county are some of the oldest features in the English landscape.

1. Rodwell W. The Origins and Early Development of Witham, Essex.1993.
2. Angus Winchester. Discovering Parish Boundaries. Shire Publications 1990
3. Hoskins W. G. The Making of the English Landscape

View from near Lynfield garage. Mature elm trees, survivors of Dutch Elm disease. Distant view of wooded Wickham Bishops ridge.

Aerial view of north east Witham, showing the Roman road, the bypass, Eastways industrial estate and the Forest Road estate. The distinctive pattern of the hedges of the 'detached' portion of the parish can be seen divided by the railway. This photo is out of date - the rather featureless fields are now the site of a golf course and thousands of trees have been planted.

4 Ancient Field Systems

Historic landscapes have for long been thought of in terms of Bronze Age barrows and stone walls on Dartmoor, or Iron Age forts in the hilly parts of Britain. But recently there has been an upsurge of interest in the history of local landscape in lowland areas.

In the 1970s and 1980s publications by Oliver Rackham[1] and Warwick Rodwell[2] demonstrated that much of the Essex landscape in general and in the Witham area in particular, was far older than had previously been thought. Their researches indicated that this local pattern of fields probably pre-dates the Romans, extending back to the early Iron Age, nearly 3000 years ago.

Aerial photography has revealed crop marks giving evidence of continuous occupation and farming for thousands of years. This is the history of settlements, parishes, boundaries, hedges, trees and traffic ways and the development of the patterns of fields and tracks, and the extent to which today's landscape can be explained by, or related to its past.

As Rodwell says:

Aerial photography and archaeological fieldwork over the past 25 years have revealed a more-or-less continuous settlement zone along the brick earth and gravel terraces of the rivers in central Essex. The Blackwater valley has been particularly productive of evidence for ring ditches, enclosed settlements and field systems, ranging in age from Bronze Age to late Roman. Although more ephemeral, evidence of Neolithic activity and early Anglo Saxon settlement is increasingly coming to light. Wherever excavations have taken place, a long history of site occupation has been established. It can be demonstrated that large tracts of ancient field systems are still preserved around these nuclei, as relict features in modern landscapes. The river valleys and their hinterlands were laid out at an early date with field systems and trackways of roughly rectilinear plan.

According to Rackham, *The Neolithic Revolution began about 4500 BC. when people arrived on these shores with farming skills, domestic animals and cereal crops and set about converting the* Wildwood *to farmland.* He estimates that by the early Iron Age in about 500 B.C. half of England had ceased to be Wildwood. A Neolithic barrow has been identified in the Rivenhall area together with a profusion of worked flints of that period and every period since.

From the time of the earliest people who walked these islands, the occurrence and orientation of rivers and streams and possible crossing places were of utmost importance. Wet and marshy areas were places to avoid. Neolithic man and his successors probably followed the tracks of animals, who would also prefer higher and drier ground, and in that way routes gradually became established.

In order to illustrate and highlight the pre-historic routes, and main river crossings, **Map 2** has been compiled. It shows clearly that the focal point of the area has been the (relative) height of Chipping Hill with its earthworks dating back to the Iron or Bronze Age, overlooking the junction of the two valleys and the principal crossing of the River Brain. It is converged upon by routes from various directions.

Lower down the River Brain at Sauls Bridge, the Maldon Road crosses and links up with the route to Maldon over the River Blackwater at Blue Mills.

Before the Roman invasion, London was a small town of little significance to the people of mid-Essex, so there was no need for a main road to go there. The main road to the west probably led to Terling. Farm production was organised for household and local consumption and generated little traffic outside the immediate area.

Rodwell has shown that the Roman Road, built in about 50 A.D. as a priority military route between Colchester and London, ignores the settlements and cuts through the fields just like a modern motorway. This can be seen particularly in the southwest corner of the parish at Witham Lodge where the road cuts through the fields at oblique angles, clipping off the corners. The conclusion must be that the fields and their boundaries predate the road.

However, to the north-east of Witham, the field boundaries in a similar field system meet the Roman Road at right angles in a more regular manner. The explanation for the difference may be that this length of the Roman Road is on the line of an older road.

Williamson[3] has shown in his work on a comparable area of the boulder clay at Yaxley in Suffolk, that the Roman Road named Pye Street, slices through the similar landscape pattern of small fields and long sinuous trackways. It was only when Roman surveyors arrived that straight lines in the landscape became possible

The original, principal routes show up as strong, sinuous lines, roughly parallel to the rivers, creating a simple layout which was further divided with lesser tracks and field boundaries. Thus was created a pattern where the lines were neither quite straight, nor quite parallel and the fields are not quite rectangular, nor even in size.

And yet when one studies the Tithe Map or a modern map there is an inescapable sense of informal order which is neither quite regular nor quite haphazard. This is the essence of an Iron Age Field System.

Field systems of this nature do not appear overnight. The fields were not just individual clearings, but adhered to an overall pattern, albeit an informal one of scattered farmsteads. They are an indication that the farming people who made them were sufficiently settled and organised over a considerable period of time to create an extensive farming system. Compact semi-regular fields suited the Iron Age farmers and their small ploughs and Britnell[4] has shown that the small fields were equally useful for

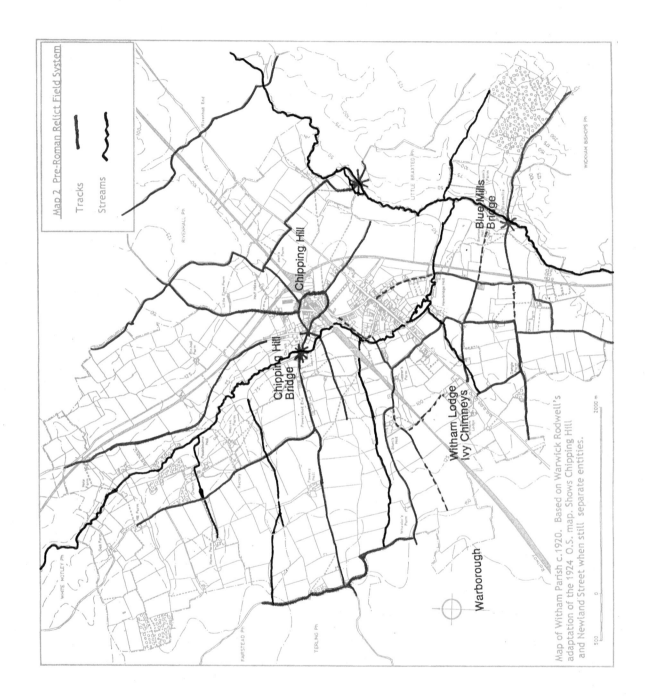

Map of Witham Parish c.1920. Based on Warwick Rodwell's adaptation of the 1924 O.S. map. Shows Chipping Hill and Newland Street when still separate entities.

Map 2 Pre-Roman Relict Field System

Tracks

Streams

Chipping Hill

Blue Mills Bridge

Chipping Hill Bridge

Witham Lodge Ivy Chimneys

Warborough

livestock without depending on common land grazing. The Romans apparently did not alter the system they found.

There are two aspects of the post-Roman period to consider. First, there is very little evidence in this part of Essex of the destruction caused elsewhere when the pagan invaders were taking the place of the Romans. Indeed, Rodwell has shown that there was continued building activity to meet agricultural needs at Rivenhall throughout the period. Secondly, there does not appear to have been mass settlement of Saxons as in Kent and East Anglia, except round the coast of Essex. It would seem that the farming system of the Iron Age changed very little in the centuries between the arrival of the Romans and the invasion by the Normans a thousand years later. The Dark Ages may have been largely unrecorded, but in Essex, it would seem that farming continued though probably at a less intense level. So the recording of an unusually high proportion of freemen in Witham working on the many small fields or crofts at the time of the Domesday may owe something to the Romans as well as the Danes.

A surprising thought! Not only are the field systems remarkable, and ancient, but even more astonishing, is the apparent continuity over more than two millennia.

At this point it is useful to add a comment from Susan Oosterhuizen: *"Cambridgeshire from the Air".*

Their survival (hedges and field systems) need not mean that these fields have been continuously farmed since they were first laid out – they may have suffered periods of neglect when they lay uncultivated and full of scrub. But farmers clearing the land for farming once again, will have found the ditches which first delineated them and will have reused them, thus unwittingly perpetuating a field pattern which pre-dates the Romans.

As Rodwell says:

The survival of these landscapes indicates that within these areas, agricultural land-use must have continued without major interruption. The very fact that it has never been found necessary to enclose or re-enclose the majority of the Essex landscape, bears testimony to the abiding maintenance of agriculture and land management systems.

The Field Systems of Witham Parish

Map 2 shows clearly that the pattern of tracks and roads is based on topographical features and focussed upon the Iron Age enclosure at Chipping Hill and the principal crossing of the River brian.. The line of the Roman road can be seen to ignore the existing layout of fields and roads and settlements.

To the north of Witham the strong sinuous lines of the parallel field boundaries are very pronounced and some of the ditches are deep and wide. These lines continue across the parish boundary towards Cressing Temple and even further towards Braintree. Southwards they continue along Forest Road and Motts Lane and down to the Blackwater River at Little Braxted Mill. Following the river south, there is a pronounced system based on Blue Mills Hill and the roads to Dengie and Pondholton Farms. It is the west end of this system which is interrupted by the Roman Road cutting through at an angle and separating it from the next system based on the Witham Lodge Iron Age Enclosure and the Ivy Chimnies religious site.

A little further north, the focal point is the Warborough Iron Age enclosure on the watershed between the field systems from Chipping Hill and Terling. From Powers Hall road there are more strong lines heading off in a north west direction and forming the framework of a system extending through the Notleys and even further towards Braintree. This is the ancient field system with a semi-regular pattern of tracks and field boundaries nearly regular, nearly parellel to the streams, all providing routes to link the scattered farmsteads with the focal points.

Summary of the Evidence for the Survival of an Iron Age landscape in Witham

Oliver Rackham defines *Ancient Countryside* as having:

- mixed hedges
- many paths and roads which are seldom straight
- many small woods
- nearly parallel field boundaries, which are sinuous, not straight
- no tradition of Open Fields
- a semi-regular pattern of fields

Witham's countryside shows all these characteristics, therefore the next consideration is the probable age of the system. Factors to consider are:

- Both the Iron Age enclosure at Witham Lodge about 250 B.C. and the Roman road about 50 A.D. are thought to have been superimposed on the field system, which must therefore be older

- Aerial photography and archaeological fieldwork show almost continuous occupation of the land from Neolithic days

- Long sections of the parish boundary follow the zig-zag pattern of the fields which must have pre-dated the parish.

- The pattern of roads and tracks follows the streams, and is focussed upon the early Iron Age landmark of the encampment at Chipping Hill and the pre-historic crossing of the river just below it

- The strong sinuous lines of the field systems, roughly parallel to the streams emphasise the semi-regular nature of the network which is typical of the Iron Age

- The absence of evidence of any fundamental re-organisation to Open Fields or subsequent Enclosures

The conclusion is the strong probability that this landscape pattern was well established before the Romans came. The farming revolution began in pre-historic times when the Neolithic settlers adopted a settled way of life and started to domesticate animals and grow crops. Aerial photography continues to discover crop marks of Iron Age and even earlier settlement, increasing the evidence that the land has been settled and farmed since at least 1000 B.C. The landscape pattern we see today remains basically as created by pre-historic farmers about 3000 years ago. A remarkable situation!

Witham in the Wider Area

Map 2 shows the field systems that lie within Witham parish, but as they were well established in the pre-Christian era, at least 1000 years before parishes were thought of, it is hardly surprising to find that they extend into what are now neighbouring parishes.

Hunter[5] writing about the parish of Cressing immediately to the north of Witham, says:

Of interest are the parallel field boundaries stretching into the parishes of Witham and Rivenhall. They respect these fields which suggests an early origin. These boundaries are shown on the 1874 O.S. map, and although there are clearly gaps, they retain a resemblance to many early field systems in archaeological surveys. They follow a ridge which parallels the Brain valley and merge into the land and field system to the north of Cressing.

Oliver Rackham in "The Local Historian" No.27/2[6] also describes these long boundaries where

Cressing Temple is in the middle of an area of parallel, but not straight, field boundaries, of a kind associated with Bronze or Iron Age landscape planning.

Similarly, there are strong lines represented by lanes and hedges to the west of the Brain valley, which although not completely continuous, could be said to extend from Witham, through the Notleys, towards Braintree. The hedges along these lines are consistently multi-species and in some places have impressive ditches, both characteristics being signs of great age.

On considering these strong boundary lines in the wider context, on maps and in the field, it seems both logical and reasonable to suggest that Witham's field system is part of a more extensive ancient system, dating back to at least 1000 B.C. and covering most of the chalky boulder clay ridge between Witham and Braintree.

This would be a pre-historic field system of at least 20 square miles!

1. Oliver Rackham The History of the English Countryside
2. Warwick Rodwell "The Origins and Early Development of Witham,Essex
3. Williamson, Tom, Parish Boundaries, Early Fields, Continuity and Discontinuity
4. Britnell R. H. The Making of Witham.
5. Hunter J. The Age of Cressing Field Boundaries
6. Rackham O. The Local Historian No.27/2

5 Major Landscape Changes Since 1839

When the Tithe Map was drawn in 1839, the Eastern Counties Railway Company had just acquired the land for the "Railroad Line" separating the two sectors of the town, Chipping Hill and Newland Street and slicing through the Iron Age Camp in the process. The map shows a tiny station, but no railway development, no sidings and no branch lines.

By 1874, when the 6" O.S. map was published, the Braintree branch line had been built and a new road, more or less parallel with it, from Rickstones Road to Hole Farm had been constructed. At the same time, the old road from the north of Church Street to Hole Farm, forming part of the parish boundary, was closed. This road can be clearly seen in aerial photographs above the river meadows, while further on it becomes visible on the ground as a hollow way with banks either side and a few very tall hawthorn bushes to indicate where the hedge line used to be. (See Front Cover)

I have not come across any explanation for this new road, but it did provide an easier route to Braintree than the rather narrow Church Street. At first, it runs parallel to the railway, crossing several fields with consequent re-organisation of the boundaries and the loss of some hedges. It is interesting that the hedges planted along the new road, and therefore datable to about 150 years old, are poor in shrub species in contrast with the other hedges in the vicinity, thereby neatly confirming the theory about dating hedges. (See section on "How old are the hedges"?)

At about the same time as the Braintree line, the Maldon branch railway was constructed (through the fields). In the following 90 years it became the limit of the town development. Since it was closed in the 1960s, the old railway line has become the dividing line between housing and the industrial estate, and now the bypass in its turn has become the limit to development.

The building of the bypass, the new A12, has been the largest construction work in Witham's history. It cuts a broad swathe through the countryside, much wider than the railways. Now in 2001, nearly all the land "in the bow of the bypass" has been developed, either with housing or industry, and the only big area left, the "Maltings Lane" site will shortly become a housing estate.

In the 1960s and 1970s the big GLC housing estates were built and the spread of the town, at least 10 times the former area, is shown on Map 3. In order of building, Templars Estate came first, followed by Forest Road, Allectus Way, Flora Road and Spa Road.

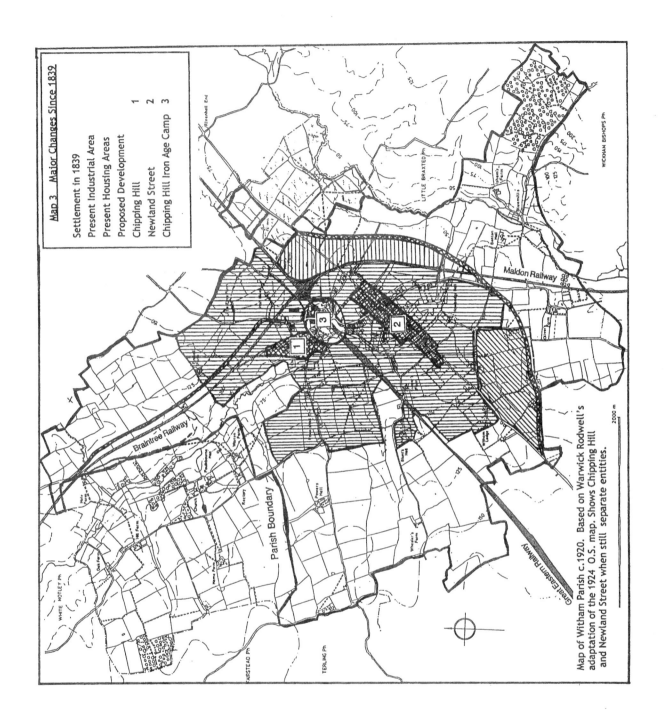

Map 3   Major Changes Since 1839

Settlement in 1839
Present Industrial Area
Present Housing Areas
Proposed Development
Chipping Hill   1
Newland Street   2
Chipping Hill Iron Age Camp   3

Map of Witham Parish c.1920. Based on Warwick Rodwell's
adaptation of the 1924 O.S. map. Shows Chipping Hill
and Newland Street when still separate entities.

At the same time, the industrial estates of Freebournes Road and Eastways were developed between the bypass and the line of the old Maldon railway. The fields on these sites have been obliterated, destroying any archaeological record they may have had. It now seem probable, according to Rodwell[1] that there was considerable evidence of past and prehistoric use, especially Bronze and Iron Age occupation of this area, as on similar nearby sites.

That record has been lost, together with virtually all the hedges which were part of the archaeological evidence. Let us hope that what remains of the historic Iron Age landscape can be better protected and preserved.

1. Warwick Rodwell. The Origins and Early Development of Witham Essex. 1993

6 The Ancient Landmark
The Parish Boundary

W. G. Hoskins[1] who pioneered the study of the English landscape, considered that boundaries, whether of parish, estate, hundred or county are some of the oldest features in the English landscape and that all such features are older than previous generations imagined.

When parishes were being created, at some time before the Norman Conquest, landowners and local dignitaries must have met to discuss the limits of their parish. When agreement had been reached, it was necessary to mark the boundary as permanently as possible, for there were no maps and very few people were literate. There have been changes over the centuries since then, but there is good reason to believe that much of the parish boundary, as it exists today is essentially the same as when first marked out.

This study is based on The Tithe Map Survey of Witham, 1839-43[2]. During those four years, the Tithe Commissioners mapped out every parish, field by field, giving the name and size and ownership of each, and adding a number. Tithes were originally one tenth of all produce or profit, but by 1839 this had been commuted to a sum of money, listed as the Tithe Rateable Value for each field. The first impression on studying the boundary, is its haphazard nature as it follows a road, but only for a short distance, and then zigzags round or across the fields, or follows a stream. In an attempt to establish any reason behind this apparently illogical situation, I have listed the natural boundaries such as streams and the semi-natural, such as roads, and tried to find explanations for the "Undefined" lengths. *See Map 1*

Tracks and Roads forming some part of the Boundary

The Roman Road	The "detached" section of Witham parish	about ¼ mile
Wickham Bishops Road	From junction with Mope Lane to Wickham Bishops crossroads	just over ½ mile
Terling Lane	West of Wheelers Farm to Dancing Dicks then to Terling Four Releet crossroads then along Peg Millars Lane, Fairstead Rd.	100 yards about ½ mile about ½ mile
Old Road to Cressing	north of Church Street to Hungry Hall,	about 1 mile
Oliver's Lane	"Green Road" northwest from Rickstones Road towards Cressing Temple about ¼ mile	

The only section in the whole length of the boundary which is straight for more than a few yards, is where the "detached" section borders on the Roman road for about ¼ mile. Otherwise the roads used, such as Oliver's Lane north of Rickstones Road, are good examples of the sinuous lines of age old tracks. Other roads are followed for very short distances only, but must nevertheless have been in existence before the boundary was laid down, and so they also form part of the ancient network: The shortness of the lengths emphasises the frequent changes of direction.

They are:

Latneys Farm	Lane running south from the Roman Road	about 200 yards
Maldon Road	south of Dengie and Olivers Farms	100 yards
Wickham Bishops	cross-roads, towards Totham	about 100 yards
Coleman's Lane	south from junction with Roman Road	200-300 yards
Motts Lane	northwest of Roman Road	200-300 yards
Faulkbourne Road	North of Devils Pit	about 200 yards
Rickstones Road	North of Elm Farm	about 200 yards

Rivers and streams forming part of the Parish boundary

In this relatively dry part of England there are not too many streams, but because of the heavy nature of the land and need for drainage, every field is (or once was) bounded by hedges with their attendant ditches and some of these were designated as the boundary. Some of the ditches, especially on the "strong, sinuous lines" of the Relict Field Systems, are impressively deep and/or wide.

The streams followed are:

River Blackwater	downstream from Little Braxted Mill	about ¾ mile
Unnamed stream	in deep ditch on the northeast side of Chantrey Wood	about ½ mile
	and again south of its junction with the Blackwater	200-300 yards
Unnamed stream	south from the Fairstead Road In the 1815 Perambulation it is called "The Great Waterfall." (Was the rainfall much greater in those days?) The same from Powers Hall to the Faulkbourne Road.	about 200 yards
		About ½ mile

Undefined Boundaries

The Tithe Map shows several fields with "undefined Boundaries", marked with dotted lines. These generally seem to indicate a previous woodland area, extending across the Parish Boundary. For instance, the northern side of Chantrey Wood is a right angled dotted line on the Witham Tithe Map, which corresponds with a dotted line on the **Little Braxted Tithe Map**[3] and both parishes show a substantial area of woodland.

Similarly, there is about half a mile of "undefined" boundary between the junction of Mope Lane with Blue Mills Hill and the River Blackwater. On **Chapman and Andre's Map**[4] of 1777 the area immediately south of this line was part of the extensive Sparkey Wood. On either side of Maldon Road there are lengths of "undefined" boundary dividing fields with "woody" names, while somewhere nearby was a 34 acre wood called Bushy Leas. In the north of the parish, Vicarage Wood was linked with the extensive wooded area of Tarecroft Wood and Rivenhall Thicks.

It seems possible in these instances that the woodland may have been shared between communities from the days of the earliest settlers, and the boundary was ill-defined, because digging a bank and ditch through woodland would have been very hard work and only undertaken if essential. When the wood was cleared for arable fields there would be no boundary earth banks to remove, and so the boundary continued to be "undefined".

However, this explanation does not seem to fit the situation across the Warren Field near Faulkbourne Hall where there is no record of any woodland. A different explanation could apply in the vicinity of Little Elms, where there were complications with the Glebe lands of Rivenhall and Cressing and the "detached" portions of Faulkbourne and Rivenhall parishes.

To summarise, in the 17½ miles of the boundary we have about 2 miles that follow streams or rivers, about 4 miles following ancient tracks and about 4 miles of "Undefined" of which about half has a clear link with woodland. The largest portion perpetuates ancient field boundaries and zigzags across the countryside for 7-8 miles. Having studied the adherence to natural or semi-natural features, one is then presented with anomalies:

Why did the boundary follow a perfectly good semi-natural feature like the "Green Road" north of Rickstones Road for only 2 fields?

Why did it follow a very well defined stream and ditch for about half the length of Chantrey Wood and then go off through the wood (the route is undefined), but join up with the same stream half a mile down, just before it flows into the River Blackwater?

North of Chipping Hill the Parish Boundary follows the old, pre-railway road, the continuation of Church Street towards Cressing. It kept on the slope above the marshy ground by the river and can be seen distinctly in aerial photographs as a crop mark. Further on it is still evident as a sunken depression with banks and ditches and some magnificent trees. It emerges under the railway bridge by Hole Farm and crosses the field on a bank to join the present road.

Why, after about 1½ miles following the same track, does the boundary then divert opposite Hungry Hall to enclose about half of the field known as **Ozhod?** This seems a particularly contrived diversion. Could it have been designed specifically to achieve the meeting up with the boundaries not only of Cressing, but also Faulkbourne and White Notley Parishes? And could the reason for this have been that it was a meeting place for the Hundred of Witham? After all, it is a natural viewpoint and roughly central to the parishes which made up the Hundred. Or was it just an awkward shape, left over when Faulkbourne parish was carved out of the Witham Hundred?

Williamson[5] says:

Persistent features of this ancient landscape are not continuously followed by parish boundaries. A parish boundary often runs along a sinuous lane for a short distance then leaves it, the lane continuing and being joined by another parish boundary further along its course. In short, the boundaries appear to have been imposed upon an earlier landscape.

Appendix: Parishes in the Hundred of Witham

Bradwell	Great Braxted	Little Braxted	Little Coggeshall	Terling
Cressing	Fairstead	Faulkbourne	Hatfield Peverel	Ulting
Kelvedon	Black Notley	White Notley	Rivenhall	Witham

1. W. G. Hoskins *The Making of the English Landscape* Hodder and Stoughton, Publishing Ltd.
2. *The Tithe Map Survey for Witham 1839-43 E.R.O. D/CT 405*
3. *Little Braxted Tithe Map E.R.O. D/CT 49*
4. *Chapman and Andre's Map of Essex 1777*
5. *Williamson Tom, Parish Boundaries, Early Fields, Continuity and Discontinuity Journal of Historical Geography*

7 Woodland

The Parish of Witham is not richly endowed with woodland and even at the time of the Tithe Map in 1839, there were only 8 woods marked. These amounted to just over 150 acres, all situated on the boundary and in the more remote parts of the Parish. Only three of these woods survive today which makes them particularly important ecologically and in the local landscape. By far the largest is Chantrey Wood on the Wickham Bishops slopes and much smaller are The Spring in the north near Whiteheads Farm, and The Grove on the Terling boundary. Map 4.

Traditionally, management of woodland in Essex has for generations, probably millennia, been by coppice and standard trees. Coppicing consists of cutting broad leaved, deciduous trees down to ground level, a process which stimulates new growths from the stump or "stool". Sections of woodland were coppiced in rotation and the resultant growth used for fodder and the small wood for fuel, fencing, tools and building.

The management of trees by coppicing can extend their life span almost indefinitely, and there are some very large and very old coppices in the parish.(See end of section on hedgerow trees.) Amongst the coppice stools, some trees would be left to grow as standards, to their full height and maturity, to provide large timber for buildings and ships.

Criteria for Ancient Woods

- The wood has a bank, with an exterior ditch to keep animals out and away from the new foliage.

- There are usually ponds within the wood

- There is a rich assortment of shrubs and trees

- The outline of the wood is sinuous, rather than straight

- There is usually evidence of pollarding and/or coppicing

- Edges of wood often form part of the Parish Boundary.

Surviving Ancient Woods in Witham

	Acres
The Spring, Whiteheads Farm	1·9
The Grove Wood Peg Millars Lane	2·7
Chantrey Wood	105·3
Total	109·9

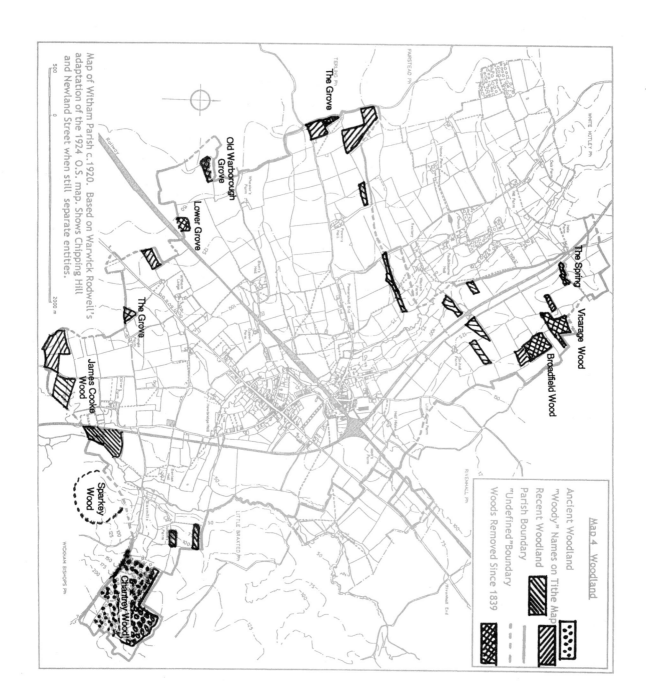

Map of Witham Parish c.1920. Based on Warwick Rodwell's adaptation of the 1924 O.S. map. Shows Chipping Hill and Newland Street when still separate entities.

Map 4 Woodland

Ancient Woodland
"Woody" Names on Tithe Map
Recent Woodland
Parish Boundary
"Undefined"Boundary
Woods Removed Since 1839

The Grove
Old Warborough Grove
Lower Grove
The Grove
James Cooke Wood
Sparkey Wood
Chantrey Wood
The Spring
Vicarage Wood
Broadfield Wood

The Spring

Situated south of Hungry Hall, this very small wood, only 1·9 acres, has a bank and external ditch all the way round, except where the new Cressing Road was taken through when the railway was built. The bank is most pronounced on the north side. There is a deep pond (although it has been dry in recent summers). The outline of the wood is sinuous (very!)

The hedge, or mixture of shrubs, along the north side contains 8 species including spindle and hazel. There is an almost pure stand of spindle at the southeast corner. The hedge on the south side also contains 8 species. There are mature trees of oak, maple, ash and elm to a height of 50' to 60'. There has been fairly recent planting of poplars inside the widest part at the eastern end.

It is worth noting that the word "Spring" seems to have been used in the "Perambulation" of 1815 as meaning a wood. I understand that originally, and perhaps more exactly, it could also have meant woodland after coppicing.

The Grove Wood

In the northwest corner of the parish, bordering on Peg Millar's Lane, is another good example of an ancient wood which is only 2·7 acres. It is just a remnant of a wood previously about 4 times as big. On the Tithe Map, parcels 687, 688 and 689 were arable fields named The Grove, so presumably they were previously part of the wood making it four times its present size.

There is a marked difference between the ancient west side and the cutback east and south sides. The west side is sinuous, has a deep and wide ditch and for most of its length a bank, whereas the east and south sides are straight with a shallow ditch and a low bank.

On the west side 11 species were found, including spindle and hazel, whereas the east side is a planted hawthorn hedge with just a few elder trees marking the new edge of the wood. At least half of the wood has been grubbed about five years ago, leaving a fringe of mixed trees; ash, oak maple and elm, up to 70' but with no notable trees.

The frequency of the name "The Grove" calls for comment. Rodwell[1] suggests that any wood called "Grove" may have had links with pre-Christian worship. On the Tithe Map there were 4 woods called "The Grove" and it is interesting that three of them, Lower Grove near Woodend Farm, Old Warborough Grove and The Grove near Dengie Farm occurred at the west end of the parish near Warborough, the site of cropmark of an Iron Age enclosure. The only survivor is The Grove in Peg Millar's Lane.

Chantrey Wood

Recorded in Domesday Book. The name probably dates from the time when St. John's Chantrey in Witham's St. Nicolas Church, was founded in 1397. It is possible that this may also be the date of its inclusion in Witham Parish. Its 105 acres would have been a valuable addition for the people of Witham. The Chantrey's endowment consisted of 2 houses, and 130 acres of arable land, meadow, pasture and woodland.

In 1988, after at least 600 years, and possibly 1000, all the land to the east of the River Blackwater, including Chantrey Wood, was transferred from Braintree District to Wickham Bishops Parish in Maldon District. An historic link broken!

Chantrey Wood occupies the west and northwest facing slope of the Wickham Bishops ridge, on London Clay, heavy and difficult to work and thereby illustrating Oliver Rackham's[2] belief that woodland, although valuable, has only been tolerated on land which is little use for anything else.

The eastern boundary of Chantrey Wood is not easy to assess, either on the Tithe Map, or now, as it consists of several little plots in private ownership. They total about 7 acres, mostly woodland or rough grazing. For convenience, I have taken them to be woodland and included them with Chantrey Wood.

The southern edge, alongside Blue Mills Hill, has the well defined ditches and wood banks of an ancient wood. The greater part of the northern edge follows a stream, for most of its length in a steep little valley. Both of these edges show the sinuous lines of ancient boundaries.

I have recently had the privilege of a conducted tour of Chantrey Wood and am able to report at first hand on the extremely sticky, slippery nature of the ground at the end of a wet February! There are wood banks and ditches and several ponds and little streams, all indications of historical changes. The new owner has commissioned a thorough ecological survey and is particularly interested in the hazel and hornbeam coppice and the wide variety of habitats that can be restored or created to enhance the remnants of the ancient wood. Good news for local bio-diversity!

Non-Surviving Tithe Map Woods

Name	Acres
Vicarage Wood, Whiteheads Farm	10·7
Part of Longland "	1·5
Broadfield Wood "	12·3
The Grove, N.W. of Dengie Farm	3·8
Lower Grove N. of Woodend Farm	2·8
Old Warborough Grove Warborough	1·8
Wood Field	2·2
Spring Field	2·0
Wood Field	3·7
Small Wood	0·2
The Spring	0·6
Total lost since 1839	41·6

(N.B. Acreages are given in decimals, NOT in acres, roods and poles!)

Lost Woods, Undefined Boundaries and Woody Names

The area of greatest loss was in the north of the parish where Vicarage Wood with part of Long Land, and Broadfield Wood, totalling 24·5 acres, have vanished. They were part of the Glebe land belonging to the Chipping Hill demesne and joined with the well wooded areas of Tarecroft Wood and Rivenhall Thicks in Rivenhall and Cressing parishes.

Their former presence is shown by "undefined" boundaries, shown as dotted lines on the Tithe Map. Judging by the species-rich records on the remaining hedges, they were probably ancient woods, though the "field" part of the name of Broadfield Wood, may indicate a planted or secondary wood.

Similarly, the northern side of Chantrey Wood is a dotted line, indicating that the wood continues in Little Braxted parish. Between Mope Lane and the River Blackwater, the dotted line indicates a former connection with Sparkey Wood, shown on Chapman and Andre's map of 1777 to be much more extensive than now.

Where the boundaries were "undefined", the use of the woodland was probably shared between parishes. Access to woodland was vital for all communities, but digging banks and ditches through woodland would have been very hard work and only undertaken if essential. So it may be that it was easier to share the woodland produce and deal with any disputed ownership in other ways. Subsequently, when the wood was cleared for arable fields, there were no earthbanks to remove, and the boundary continued to be"undefined".

Fields with "Woody" names such as 8 Acre Wood, were most likely to have been actual wood, not too far back in time. Witham and Hatfield Peverel Tithe Maps[3] show adjoining fields with "Woody" names and there was a 34 acre wood called Bushy Leas in this vicinity.

Near to Peg Millar's Lane were previous sections of the Grove Wood, First Wood Field and Further Wood Field. Near to Wood End Farm was Wood Field while south of Oliver's Farm was a group of fields: Lower, 7 and 8 Acre Woods, Wood Lye and Wood Pightle, overlapping into Hatfield Peverel parish.

On the evidence of these field names, nearly 97 acres of woodland was lost at some time before 1838. To put it in context, that is an area nearly as big as Chantrey Wood. Woodland clearance is nothing new! The present state of woods in the parish is that the area of woodland lost since 1839 is almost equal to the area gained.

The Removal of Vicarage Wood in 1841

I am grateful to Tom Henderson for the following extract from a document in the Essex Record Office[4] giving the circumstances of the removal of the Vicarage Wood.

Faculty given for converting certain woodland belonging to the Glebe of Witham Vicarage into Arable Land. The wood is of very inferior nature and the land is uncongenial to the growth of either Timber or underwood.

Having carefully examined the state of the Vicarage House domestic and agricultural buildings and fences and finding much required to be done to put the same in substantial repair my attention was called to the woodland for the supply of timber necessary for such repairs when I found that the timber in the nine acre wood was so small and unthrifty and the soil so uncongenial to the growth of either timber or underwood that I without hesitation recommend that the same be stubbed and Timber or other materials for the substantial repair of the fences exchanged for that felled in the Glebe Wood and the land converted to arable culture.

The wood lies detached from the other Vicarial glebe and is subject to constant depredation. (Vandalism in 1841?!)

The total value was £185. That was the end of Vicarage Wood! But its legacy remains with us as some of the most varied hedges in the parish.

This seems to have been a report to the Vicar and presumably it was acted upon because the wood had become an arable field by the time of the 1874 map.

Woodland Planted since 1950

	Estimated Acres
The Warren Warren Farm	2·0
Broom Field " "	0·2
Balls Field " "	3·0
pt. Valley Field North Witham	2·0
pt. 8 Acre Bradley "	2·0
pt. Little Godman "	2·2
pt. Bradleys "	2·0
Little Tutty Powers Hall	3·0
The Community Woodland	
"James Cooke Wood"	8·0
Total	24·4

The new plantings are mostly quite prominent shelter belts or screening which are already adding considerably to the quality of the landscape.

Secondary Woodland

Fair Bottom E. of R. Blackwater	5·0
Footpath Field "	1·0
Lower River Field S. of Olivers Farm	5·0
Total	11·0

On land that is left uncultivated and ungrazed, or only partly grazed, trees will seed and spread naturally and grow, and eventually woodland which is described as secondary, will take over. In such a wood there will be a mixture of species but no indication of the regular lines of a plantation. Since 1839, about 11 acres of secondary woodland has arisen and a further 24 acres of new woodland has been planted. Together they add up to about 35 acres roughly the same as the amount lost in the same period

It must be emphasised again, that replacement woodland, however great the mixture of species planted, the richness and diversity of flora and fauna of a genuine ancient wood cannot be replaced. Now that Chantrey Wood is no longer in this parish, the sum total of ancient woodland is only 4·6 acres. Therefore these few acres of ancient woodland which have survived, are particularly important.

Summary of Woodland

Former woodland,
"Woody" names pre-1839	97 acres
Woods on 1839 Tithe Map	151 acres
Tithe map woods surviving in 2001	118 acres
Woods lost between 1839 and 2001	33 acres
New Planting	24 acres
Secondary woodland	11 acres

1. Warwick Rodwell. The Origins and Early Development of Witham,Essex 1993
2. Oliver Rackham. The History of the Countryside Orion Books Ltd. 1986
3. E.R.O.D/CT 405 Tithe Map Survey Witham E.R.O. D/CT 167 Tithe Map Survey Hatfield Peverel
4. E.R.O.D/P 30/3/2/. Faculty given 25th.March 1841

Aerial view of Warborough showing the A12, Woodend Farm, the main east coast railway, and the clear crop mark of a rounded rectangular Iron Age enclosure.

Olivers Lane. Ancient track with dense multi-species hedges. The first stretch is, however, dominated by blackthorn, shown in full flower.

8 Field Names

The subject of field names is fascinating. They are so varied, so evocative, and sometimes so revealing of the unrewarding nature of their soil. Rather than attempt to discuss all the field names, those of the fields adjacent to the parish boundary about 25% of the total, have been taken as a representative sample. They can be divided into groups:

Group			
	1	28	descriptive or named for their location
	2	22	with historic or strange names
	3	17	woodland or former woodland
	4	15	named for their size or shape
	5	14	personal names
	6	5	crofts or smallholdings
	7	5	domestic
	8	4	very vague e.g. part of 12 Acres

1 Descriptive

The first group of names often indicate the quality of the land.

Small Gains	poor stony soil
Ozier Ground	where it was wet enough for willow beds.
The Moors	seems to have been a name used for rough grazing for livestock throughout the year, unlike the meads and meadows which were kept for the all important crop of hay for winter feed.
Broom, Furze or Sandpit Fields	light, hungry soils
Cloddy Pieces (Clotty)	heavy to work (the name speaks for itself)
Valley, Hilly, River Fields,	(the names speak for themselves)

2 Historic

The second group contains the most intriguing names with historic links, or those which seem to have no readily discernible meaning, but are nevertheless evocative of former times and people, and happenings long ago. For instance:

The Warren	An enclosure for farming rabbits, an important source of food in medieval times.
The Hollow Ground	Olivers Farm Nurseries may contain an old "hollow way" for which there was some indication on the Tithe Map.

Burghey Brook	Follows the little stream of the same name and is adjacent to the area known as The Burgh at Rivenhall End. This name is given great significance by Rodwell as being the possible site of the "Saxon Burgh" built in 912 as a defence against the Vikings by King Edward the Elder.
10 Acre Breech	Harks back to a large Tudor house called Breech House
Allaker	I have found no explanation of this curious name.
Pilgrim's Croft	A tiny patch at the cross roads at the top of Wickham Bishops Hill must surely have had some connection with The Chantrey which also gave its name to the Wood.
Slooping Elm	The next door field. Was it just a strangely shaped tree?

Still in the same group, in the Rickstones Road area we have Sewlands and Crotch Fields and at the other end of the parish, opposite Lynfield Motors, the name Weather Walls tests the imagination. Cowhill Ley and Further Cowhills sound delightfully rural, but what of Third Moseley; possibly a personal name?

Then there are two names which really tease: Little Tutty, a wood behind Powers Hall, and the most evocative of all, Ozhod, the field opposite Hungry Hall. For me the name conjures up the long gone Knights Templar, but it is called Oxshots on an estate map of Cressing Temple lands of about 1300, so it may have a more mundane connection as grazing for oxen!

And there is the group of fields all bearing the name Warborough: Lower, Further, Middle and Old Warborough Grove, plus Warborough Wood, and Great Old Warborough. Rodwell suggests that the name means "watch hill". There is cropmark evidence of an Iron Age rectangular enclosure and hut circles on the watershed between Witham and Hatfield Peverel and right on the parish boundary. As far as I know there has been no excavation as yet.

Whatever Warborough was, it was very important, so important that the boundary actually shows a slight deviation to accommodate the crop mark. We are left with a legacy of about 95 acres with Warborough names on the Witham side of the boundary, plus another 20 or so acres on the Hatfield Peverel side. Also of interest is the siting of two "Grove" names at either side of the Warborough area.

3   "Woody" names

The next biggest group contains all the "woody" names, an indication of the extent of woodland in the parish at the time of the Tithe Map, or sufficiently within the historic context so that the names remain, even though the woods themselves have been grubbed.

4   Size or Shape

The fourth group consists of the least imaginative names, merely describing the size or shape of the field: e.g. 11 acres, Long Mead or Middle Field. One wonders whether these were always so, or the people who worked the land had more familiar names for them.

5   Personal Names

Perhaps the most interesting are the names in the fifth group, remembering the ownership of the land or commemorating some part of local history. Church Fields and Vicarage Wood near Hungry Hall, were owned by the Vicar, as part of the Glebe Land. They were some distance from the Vicarage and may be evidence of the widespread holdings and former power and wealth of the Church.

Goodmans, Thornhams, Harts, Goslings, Stevens, Jacksons, Gibbons, Balls and Sparkey as personal names attached to fields, commemorate people who thereby achieve some degree of immortality, for many of them have otherwise disappeared into history leaving no other trace. Where 17th century maps exist they often show the same names, though with spelling variations. For instance, "de Thornhams" occurred frequently in names in the Middle Ages so one may speculate that "Thornham" was a local place.

6   Crofts or Smallholdings

The sixth group, the names of crofts or smallholdings are revealing in that they illustrate a particular aspect of the landscape history of Witham. At the time of Domesday Witham had 7 manors, an unusually high number and again a reflection on the high proportion of freemen and small landowners. They were:

The Manor of Witham, divided into Chipping Hill and Newland and by far the largest at 5 hides (a hide was nominally about 120 acres, usually of tilled ground)

The Manors of Powershall, Blunts Hall, Howbridge, Benton Hall, Ishams.

In the thirteenth Century, a large proportion of the population of Witham were smallholders with fewer than 8 acres of land. Whether they were compact or scattered, the ownership of a small number of acres, fostered independence and allowed men to earn part of their living away from the big estates. (Source Britnell[1])

There were two terms most commonly used in the Witham area to describe compact units of arable land: field and croft. Fields tended to be above 12 acres and crofts below, but there was considerable overlap. "Land" was also used as in "Longelond". There are 5 crofts in my list: Crooked, Bell, Pear Tree, Further Green and Hither Green.

It is fascinating to realise that this aspect of land history may have had a direct influence on the landscape we see today. In other parts of the country with large estates, their size was possibly a factor in the establishment of the Open Field system. Where this happened it became the basis of farming and must have led to a considerably different way of life. With shared Open Fields there had to be much more agreement about farming operations than between individual smallholders. In order to produce crops for the community there was necessarily curtailment of individual choice of methods.

Whatever the reason, the Open Field system did not take root in this part of Essex. So the pattern of small, nearly regular, nearly rectilinear fields still with us today, is an amazing, visible, historic, link with the small farmers of 1000 years ago at the time of the Danelaw and back again to the Iron Age farmers of 2000 years ago.

7   Domestic

The group of domestic names are small fields such as Barn Field, close to the farm and dwellings. They may have been small fields, but would have been very important economically because they could be kept under close observation. A very ordinary sounding name such as Barn Field may in fact be historical and indicate a long demolished barn.

8   The final group is the collection of vague names such as "part of 8 Acres". Such evidence of split fields may well have significance which is not yet apparent.

I am grateful to Tom Henderson for the following notes:

- An "acre" was historically a strip of tilled land (typically measuring 4 rods by 40 rods).

- An "acre" was not necessarily a compact area in one enclosure. Twelve acres might be dispersed among many fields. This comment would have been more relevant in an area of the Open Field System.

- A "croft" was typically an enclosed field, held separately.

- A meaning of "land" was a strip of tilled ground and in medieval times was often used in that sense.

So we can see in this very brief summary, that field names reflect every aspect of local history: previous land tenure, ownership, classification and use, as well as commemorating many long departed people.

1. R. H. Britnell Agriculture in a Region of Ancient Enclosure 1185 - 1500. Notts. Medieval Studies Vol. 27 1983.

9 Hedgerow Trees

Looking from any viewpoint round Witham, it becomes clear that without the hedges and hedgerow trees there would be very little to engage the eye. Woodland is a very small percentage of the landscape and most of what we can see is actually outside our parish. As in other gently rolling landscapes, the pattern of fields, hedges and hedgerow trees *is* the landscape.

The hedgerow trees are the real glory of this countryside. Since the death of most of the elms, the principal trees are oaks which with their sturdy limbs and strong outlines provide the shape and texture of the landscape in this part of Essex. It is good to record that at the Terling end of the parish, hedgerow oaks have been regularly planted and after 30 or 40 years, they are becoming significant in the landscape. A splendid contribution to the countryside of today and for the future.

Trees

Elm

It is good to report that there are actually a few large elms surviving in 2 areas in the west of the parish, just enough to remind us of the splendour of their outlines in nearly every hedge before Dutch Elm Disease struck. There are now two or three schemes across the country and in Essex, attempting to propagate the survivors. It is very much to be hoped they are successful and that soon there will be replacement elms to add their most distinctive shapes to the Essex scene.

Oak

The most common hedgerow tree. Every size and shape from newly planted saplings, to some magnificent specimens fully in their prime reaching anything up to 100' tall, and 15' girth making their own very characteristic contribution to the Essex landscape. Also very important in landscape terms are the pollards.

There are also many 'stag-headed' trees, trees which have partly died back, usually as a result of drought. It is important to remember that they are not dead, and still have their own particular contribution to make as habitats for a wide range of wildlife.

Field Maple

Maples are not often great trees, but there are numerous specimens up to about 60' high. Along with oak, field maple really does seem to be the typical tree of this area and it is only when one goes further north in England that one realises how much they are typical of Essex.

Particularly as a hedgerow shrub, field maple is rich in autumn colour and its seeds provide a good source of food for wildlife.

I found just one specimen of pollarded field maple, not as far as I am aware, on a parish or other boundary, so one wonders why it was treated in this way. (Another item to revisit.)

Hawthorn

Mostly present in the hedges as a shrub species, but there are occasional trees up to about 30' high with gnarled and twisted trunks, wonderful blossom in Spring, and colour in Autumn. They are also a good source of food for over-wintering birds. Some of the hawthorn is the 'Midland' or 'Woodland' hawthorn, but I have not kept figures for this. A revision job!

Ash

Less frequent than the above but there are a few very tall trees. Perhaps more impressive are the occasional coppice stools, up to 12' across.

Hornbeam

Found in only 2 places in the survey, both in association with former woods.

Crab Apple

Occurs here and there, usually mixed in with hazel, to remind us that hedges were a most important source of food for our ancestors. Nowadays, apart from blackberries and (occasionally sloes to flavour the gin!), the harvest of the hedges is left mostly for the birds and wildlife. As so many hedges have disappeared, the importance of this depleted food supply to the rapidly dwindling numbers of birds cannot be over emphasised.

Small leaved lime

It was particularly interesting to look for the small leaved lime, the Pry Tree. The name "pry" is very old, but the derivation is not known.

Oliver Rackham[1] describes it as:

a lovely and uncommon tree of ancient woodland

a living link with Mesolithic times

very rare in hedges even in limewood areas, the exceptions are hedges which are the ghost outlines of former woods.

In this survey it was found in only two places, one definitely associated with former woodland and the other near an "undefined" boundary and therefore likely to have been former woodland.

Other species

Two species conspicuous by their absence are holly and beech. I found only one beech and two hollies in the whole area and all were near gardens indicating a possible source of seed or perhaps someone planted them!

There are just a few uncommon yet splendid specimens: a large sycamore near Mope Wood, and a wild pear near Hungry Hall which is absolutely magnificent in full bloom.

There are a few lines of cricket bat willows with their silvery leaves, following the lines of the rivers or ditches. They are now a very typical feature in the Essex landscape, but were probably not grown in commercial plantations in the days of the 1815 perambulation.

Pollards

Pollarding, cutting off all the shoots or branches of a tree at 8'-12' above the ground, is a method of obtaining a crop of poles growing at too high a level for cattle and deer to reach the new young shoots. The pollards provided a valuable crop of poles and provided wood for many purposes and for fuel.

The pollarded trees, or pollards, are something quite special. They are nearly all oaks now, but in 1815 there were about twice as many elm pollards. Most of the elms have succumbed to Dutch Elm Disease, but I was just in time with the earliest part of my survey to find some of the huge dead stumps to show where they had been and to indicate our loss. Pollards with their fantastic shapes, whether still in full vigour or in gradual decline, provide a living link with history. The bigger specimens must be several hundred years old. I am indebted to Tom Henderson for the following information:

A pollard oak cut down in 1987 near Powers Hall had a girth of 17 ft. and the pollard branches were 1 ft. in diameter. Although it was hollow, a partial count was possible and there were 168 annual rings at 12 rings to the inch. If this reflected the general rate of growth throughout the life of the tree, it would have been about 420 years old. Indeed, it was probably the oldest living thing in Witham!

Now that we have first class maps, pollards are no longer needed as boundary "marks". With very little livestock in this part of the country there is no need to grow crops of poles up in the air to protect them from hungry animals. One wonders whether the practice of pollarding will decline. Pollards are very long lived, but if no new ones are created, they will eventually disappear and something very distinctive will be lost to the Essex scene. In addition, the nooks and crannies of pollards provide a particular kind of habitat, and if we are serious about maintaining bio-diversity then there is a particularly strong case for keeping up the tradition.

The "Perambulation" of 1815 mentions at least 5 pollards used as 'marks' where there are still pollards today. It could well be that these 5 or 6 are the same trees which were "Marked "in 1815, nearly 200 years ago.

Coppicing

Coppicing is a way of making use of the self-renewing power of native broad-leaved trees. All the growths of a deciduous tree are cut down to ground level, resulting in new growth from around the stumps. The new growth is rapid and can usually keep ahead of the depredations of rabbits and hares, but deer can be a problem.

The product is a crop of poles, suitable for many purposes. This cutting down can be repeated many times, prolonging the life of the tree almost indefinitely. The resultant group of stumps is called a stool. Some of them grow to immense size and may be several hundred years old. The effect of coppicing on the ground flora can be dramatic displays of flowers as letting in the light restores life to the woodland floor.

Some species occur as shrubs within the hedge but not as standards. Whether this is due to direct management or natural ways of growth is not always clear.

In several areas the hedges have been left to grow recently with just side trimming, to create tall windbreaks, a practice which seems to emphasise their distinctive, sinuous lines.

Notable trees in the Parish

Field and/or Situation	Tree	Height
Ozhod	oaks	40-50"
Hungry Hall	pear	40"
Oliver's Lane	pollard oaks field maple tree belt oaks	 up to 60" to 40 ft.
Detached section	oak	50'
near Burgy Brook	bat willows	
On golf course over-looking Blue Mills	sycamore	70'
Near Latneys, just outside parish	2 elms (living) the smallest pollard	60' 15"
Near Wood End Farm	oaks	to 60'
Near Warborough	oaks, maple and ash hornbeams	40-50'

Pollards

Near Chantrey Wood on corner of parish	oak pollard	
Near River Blackwater on corner of parish	huge pollard oak	
South of Dengie Farm	dead elm pollards	3' dia
Near Latneys	smallest pollard oak	15' tall
Near Warborough	oak pollard	3' dia
Corner of parish Peg Millars Lane one of the 1815 "marks"?	oak pollard	60'

Notable Tree Stools in the Parish

North of Oliver's Lane	elm and oak	3' dia
	ash and hazel	10' long
Burgy Brook/Detached Section	dead elm	4' dia
	oak and field maple	3' dia
South of Dengie farm	ash stools	6' dia
	elm and field maple to	3' dia
Near Chantrey Wood	oak	12' dia

1. Dr. Oliver Rackham The History of the Countryside. Orion Books Ltd.1986

Chipping Hill from the air. The focal point of earliest development. A hilltop site overlooking the principal river crossing. Iron Age enclosure, possibly a Bronze Age site. Note the shape of the churchyard and the Old rectory garden.

Pollarded oak in Meg Millars Lane. Probably the tree 'marked' at 'Beating the Bounds' in 1815.

10 How Old Are The Hedges?

One of the main aims of this survey has been to record the hedges of the Parish, especially those on the boundary and to see what information could be established regarding their age and diversity of species.

In addition to studying maps and documentary evidence, there is an empirical method of determining the age of hedges devised by Dr. Max Hooper[1] at Monks Wood Research Station. This involves counting the number of woody species in a 30 yard length of hedge. The number of separate species identified is the approximate age of the hedge in centuries. Thus a hedge containing 5 woody species would be about 500 years old. This method has to be used in conjunction with other information, but as a "rule of thumb" can provide useful field information about hedges and the landscape.

Hooper's Theory that the older the hedge the more species it contains is based on:

- Observation of hedges whose age is known

- The observation that a hedge acquires further species as it get older

- The belief that the older hedges were planted with mixed species

- Enclosure Act hedges were nearly always planted with hawthorn only

- The understanding that the older a hedge, the more likely it is to be a woodland relic rather than planted.

The information recorded included:

- the number of shrubby species

- the number and species of climbers eg. clematis though this has not been included in the species count

- standard and pollard trees

- coppice stools and big dead stumps

- differences in level (lynchets)

- presence of ditches and ponds

37 of the Witham Parish Boundary hedges have been sampled and 153 of the remaining or internal hedges, 190 in total. When counting a long hedge it was often sampled more than once, and the samples may have shown different counts of species. The **average of the counts** for that hedge was the figure used.

It was found that:

65% of all hedges are 4 or more centuries old (76% on the boundary)

31% of all hedges are 6 or more   "   (46%   "   "   )

Put another way, 2 out of 3 of all our hedges date back to Queen Elizabeth the First, 1 out of 3 date back to The Knights Templar and 13 may date back to the Norman conquest! *An historic landscape indeed!*

Chart 1 and Table 1 show the percentage of all the hedges which showed 1-9 species. The highest percent is in the range from 3 to 6 species. The average number of species for all hedges was **4·3** giving a probable age of **4** centuries.

Table 1 Showing the number of species/30 yards

No. of species	1	2	3	4	5	6	7	8	9
% of hedges containing above no.									
of species in *all* hedges	8	8	18	19	14	18	8	3	2
in internal hedges	9	8	20	20	14	16	7	3	2
in boundary hedges	3	8	14	16	14	24	14	5	3

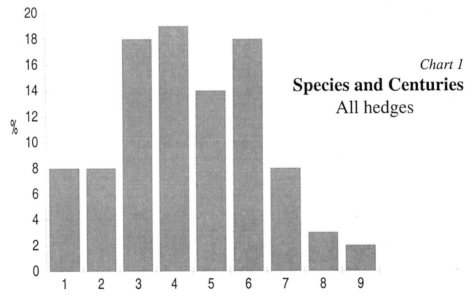

Chart 1
Species and Centuries
All hedges

One of the aims in recording the counts for hedges has been to see if there was any difference between hedges on the parish boundary and those inside the parish. If the suppositions were right about the origin of the parish and before that of the field system, then the boundaries should show more species and therefore greater age.

Chart 2 does appear to show just that. The boundary hedges do indeed have more species than the internal hedges. The average boundary hedge has 5 species and is probably 5 centuries old. This supports the theory that the boundary, once established, was more likely to remain as a long term feature.

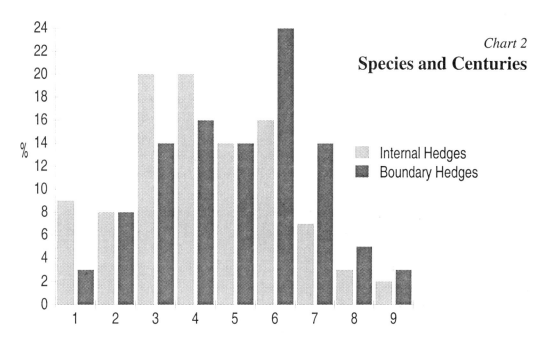

Chart 2

Species and Centuries

Internal Hedges
Boundary Hedges

Shrub Species in other Parishes

For comparison with other parishes I have used figures extracted from Hunter and Rodwell[2]. I have attempted to compare the species counts of the hedges in the parish of Rivenhall and on Bovingdon Hall Farm, and these figures are shown in Table 2.

Table 2 Comparison of Species Counts on Different Sites

Number of Species and Centuries	1-4	5-6	7+
Percentage of species counts for:			
Bovingdon Hall	27	43	29
Rivenhall	50	37	12
Witham	54	32	14

Chart 3 shows that Bovingdon Hall has the greatest percentage in the 7 or more range, whereas Rivenhall has the highest middle range of 5 to 6 and Witham has most in the 1 to 4 group. This is an indication that Bovingdon Hall Farm seems to be in a class of its own as an ancient field and hedge system. Rivenhall and Witham are basically similar, and any differences could be due to the hedge selection on different farms. Though not so rich in species as Bovingdon, the hedges of Rivenhall and Witham, are nevertheless consistent with an ancient field system. There is no evidence in the hedge counts for enclosure and the widespread planting of new hedges in the last 200 years.

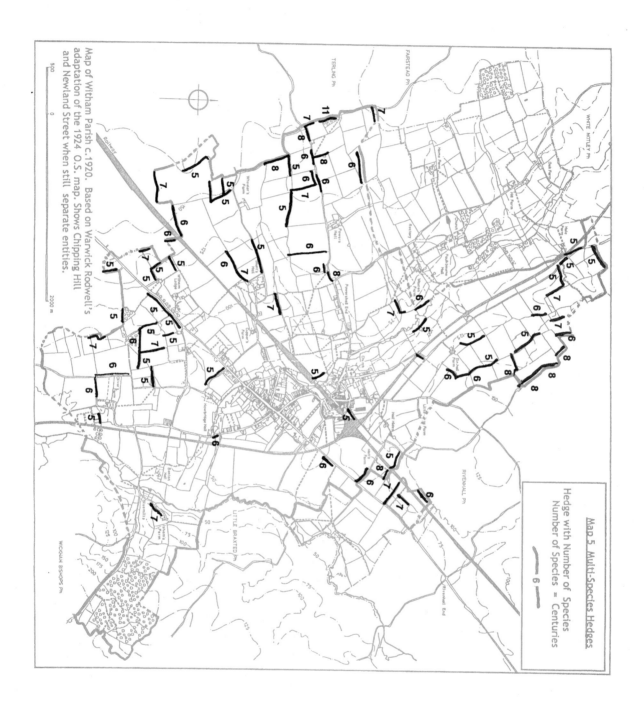

Map 5. Multi-Species Hedges

Hedge with Number of Species
Number of Species = Centuries

—— 6 ——

Map of Witham Parish c.1920. Based on Warwick Rodwell's adaptation of the 1924 O.S. map. Shows Chipping Hill and Newland Street when still separate entities.

Page 58

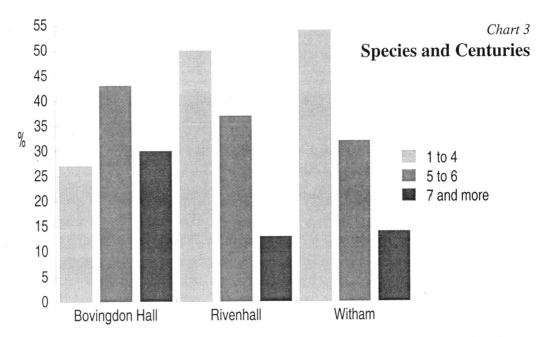

Chart 3

Species and Centuries

1 to 4
5 to 6
7 and more

Bovingdon Hall   Rivenhall   Witham

One of the limitations of Hooper's Theory is that the maximum number of hedge species which will grow naturally and self-propagate differs in various neighbourhoods. In this area, the limit would appear to be about 11 or 12 species, so however old the hedge, it will not show on this test, to be more than about 1000 years old.

Where are the Old Hedges? Links with woodland?

Map 5 shows the location of the most varied hedges, those with 5 or more species and Map 4 shows the areas where woodland survives or where it has been in the past. The two maps were studied to see if there was a link between the two factors.

It can be seen that there are clusters of species-rich hedges in the areas near:

> Whiteheads Farm,
> Maltings Lane Development Site,
> Wood End Farm,
> Warborough
> The Grove Wood in Peg Millars Lane.

In each area there are existing woods and/or there have been woods in the past, which seems to prove the link between species-rich hedges being near to woodland sources of seed.

In addition it was found that near Whiteheads Farm there are some of the most impressive and long "sinuous lines" of field boundaries and tracks running north west/south east here. They show lines of species-rich hedges with ancient spreading ash stools, large old tree stumps, deep ditches and ponds. All these are characteristics of ancient fields and hedges.

Another interesting area for rich hedges is the "detached" portion of the parish, north of the Roman road and now divided by the railway. There is no obvious link with woodland past or present here, but there are tall hedgerow trees, mostly oak, and 6-8 species in each hedge. Extra interest is provided by the ditches which are unusually deep, appearing to be deeper than needed purely for drainage.

It would seem that there is a very clear link between past and/or present woodland; and the hedges with the most species. The significant factor is probably the proximity of an abundant seed supply from the woods.

Map 5 shows only too clearly the absence of hedges in the developed areas, but even so there are a few fragments left to indicate what has been lost.

An unknown factor in the north of the parish, is in what way the landscape was affected by by the Knights Templar. They were big landowners and much of their wealth was obtained from sheep. With mixed stock as well, they would have kept good stockproof hedges. Maybe they planted new hedges or maybe they repaired the old. Of course, any new hedges they planted would now be about 600 years old.

Where are the Old Hedges?
Links with Field Systems?

Having studied the number of species and identified the approximate age of the hedges, the next consideration is whether there is any link beween age of hedge and distribution. Map 5 shows each hedge with 5 or more species and demonstrates quite clearly they are consistently widespread across the parish.

Rodwell's proposition is that both sides of the Brain Valley from the Roman Road towards Faulkbourne and the Notleys on the west, and towards Cressing on the east, are part of the pre-Roman relict landscape. John Hunter draws particular attention to the pattern of strong sinous lines of field boundaries and hedges north of Witham near Whiteheads Farm, as mentioned above. Wherever it has been possible to identify these features and where a hedge count has been made, the figures have been inserted on Rodwell's map. (Map 5).

There is a clear correlation between the pattern of ancient tracks and field boundaries, with the high species counts. It is not possible to establish the age of the field system just from the number and type of species-rich hedges. However, the coincidence of two factors, the hedges and the field pattern, would seem to reinforce the antiquity of them both.

The Diversity of Species

When counting the number of species in a hedge, where there was more than 1 count per hedge, the **average** number was taken as being most relevant and was used to estimate the age of that hedge.

However, in recording the frequency of occurrence of **each** species, **all** the samples were used. It was felt that the frequency or rarity of each species was of interest and therefore where there was more than one count per hedge, each count was recorded and used in the calculations. As many counts were made as possible in the time available and given the distances to cover.

Altogether **202** hedges were visited and **355** counts made with a total of **1549** species found, giving an average of **4·3 species per count**. (See Table 3 and Chart 5.)

Table 3 Frequency of Species at Witham in %

	All hedges	Internal	Boundary
Ash	3	3	3
Blackthorn	15	15	15
Crab Apple	3	2	4
Dogwood	4	4	5
Elder	9	9	9
Elm	12	12	11
Field Maple	14	14	15
Hawthorn	14	15	10
Hazel	8	8	10
Oak	7	6	9
Rose	1	9	5
Spindle	8	2	2
Others	2	1	2

This method of recording was devised as a practical solution to the scale of this survey. It is somewhere between Michael Astor's[3] survey of Rivenhall Parish for Warwick Rodwell, where he selected a 30 yard stretch from a distance in order to avoid bias, and the scheme carried out on the Bocking estate where every hedge was sampled and recorded every 30 yards.

Chart 4 shows that for Witham, four woody shrubs occurred most frequently, in 11% to 15% of the counts. They were **blackthorn, elm, field maple and hawthorn.** In Oliver Rackham's[3] "Planned Countryside," for example in Cambridgeshire and

Chart 4

**Frequency of Species
in Witham**

All Hedges

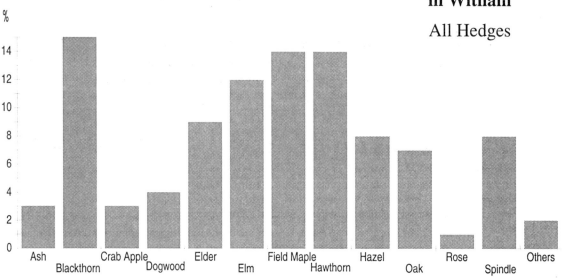

Huntingdonshire the predominant species is hawthorn, but in Essex the dominance is shared with the three other species in roughly equal shares.

In the single species hedges, 50% were pure elm, 20% each of hawthorn and blackthorn. I was rather surprised to find 2 pure hazel hedges. They showed evidence of repeated coppicing which may have favoured the hazel.

Chart 4 shows another group of four species occurring at medium frequency in 5 to 9% of the counts. These are **elder, hazel, oak and rose.**

Elder and rose are quick to move in to colonise new hedges but tend to get smothered. Hazel and oak are slow to colonise except in the vicinity of a good woodland source of seed, and can therefore be regarded as **indicators** of ancient woodland and older hedges.

The last group of shrubs, those present in less than 5% of the counts are perhaps the most interesting. Through examination of many dated hedges, it has been established by Hooper and Rackham that **crab apple, dogwood and spindle** at the lower end of the scale, together with the slightly more common **oak and hazel**, are typical of old mixed hedges. They are unlikely to occur naturally in the younger hedges because they are poor colonisers and their ability to spread depends on the proximity to ancient woodland and good seed sources. Therefore, the presence of one or more of these shrubs is highly significant as an indicator of age.

Other species occasionally present are guelder rose, pussy willow and wild plum or bullace. Both hornbeam and small leaved lime were found in only 2 places, at opposite ends of the parish, and on the fringe of former woodland. I did not find any beech except where it had obviously been planted, and only one holly tree. Nor did I find any wild service trees.

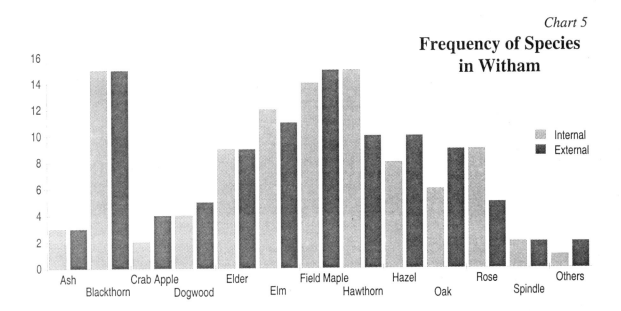

Chart 5

Frequency of Species in Witham

I looked for any difference in the number or type of species which might be related to soil or drift geology. Unfortunately in this context, there are only a few hedges left on the gravels of the Blackwater valley where development has been concentrated. Wherever possible they were sampled and seem to fit into the same widespread parish pattern.

Field maple deserves a special mention. I did not find it occuring as a single species hedge, but it is never less than 10% in any of the other hedges. This may be an indication of its success on the chalky boulder clay, but it definitely establishes field maple as the typical hedge shrub in this area. Oliver Rackham[4] regards field maple as indicative of hedges at least of Tudor age.

This factor, combined with the almost universal presence of field maple, seems to be firm evidence of a consistently old pattern of hedges.

The species counts show that two thirds (65%) of all the hedges counted in the parish contained 4 or more species and were therefore likely to be four or more centuries old. i.e. Tudor. An impressive total.

Chart 5 shows the frequency of species in internal hedges compared with those on the boundary. The only significant difference is with hawthorn which occurs in 15% of the internal hedges but in only 9% of the boundary hedges. These figures do support the idea of the greater diversity and therefore age of the boundary hedges. Newer hedges are more likely to be dominated by hawthorn and indeed this is shown particularly in a stretch planted in London Road about 20 years ago where the bend was straightened out. The adjacent remaining length provides a neat contrast with four species.

The connection between the number of species and the age of a hedge

Why should it be that the more mixed a hedge is, the older it is likely to be?

Species-rich hedges probably originate from:

- woodland relic hedges
- planting with a single species when woodland was abundant as a seed source for colonisation
- planting with mixed shrubs (probably taken from mixed woods.)
- or, a mixture of all three origins.

It is impossible to say which species-rich hedge originated in which way but natural or active coppicing ensures continuity of the shrubs with gradual replacement of old parts with new and gradual colonisation by other species at a rate determined by proximity to woodland.

Summary

- The average hedge in the Parish of Witham, contains 4·3 species and is probably at least 400-500 years old.
- The species most commonly occurring in that average hedge are blackthorn, field maple, hawthorn and elm, in roughly equal proportions.
- There are also significant percentages of oak and hazel, crab apple, dogwood and spindle, which are all regarded regarded as indicators of old hedges.
- There is remarkable consistency of such hedges across the parish.

The large number and variety of species and their wide and consistent distribution, are all features of ancient landscape and all the findings of this survey appear to support Rodwell's proposition of a pre-Roman relict landscape and to be in line with Rackham's descriptions of ancient hedges and landscapes.

1. E. Pollard, M.D. Hooper and N.W. Moore Hedges. New Naturalist Series 1974
2. Rodwell. Rivenhall:Investigations of a Villa, Church and Village.1950-1977
3. Michael Astor for Rodwell W.J. and K.A. Rivenhall, Investigations of a Vila, Church and Village
4. Oliver Rackham The Historyof the English Countryside Orion Books Ltd. 1994

11 Hedge Removal

We may think that in Witham we live surrounded by a rural landscape, rich in trees and hedges but my survey revealed that we have lost some 70% of the hedges shown on the Tithe Map of 1839, and that they are still being cut down at an alarming rate, as shown below.

Table 4 Lengths of Hedges Lost (in miles)

Date	Original Hedges	Lost to Agriculture	Lost to Development	Total Losses	Remaining Hedges
1839	18				
1955		3	3	6	12
1997		2	5	7	5
Total: Miles:		5	8	13	
Percentage:		30%	42%	72%	28%

The figures in Table 4 and Chart 6 were established by taking a random sample (see Appendix) of 39 fields on the Tithe Map and measuring their hedge lengths in 1839, again in 1955 (before most of the post-war development took place) and again in 1997.

The two main reasons for hedge removal have been changes in farm practice, and development. In the 116 years between 1839 and 1955, 6 miles, or 33%, of the original 18 miles were removed. This was almost equally due to field enlargement and development, each at some 3 miles.

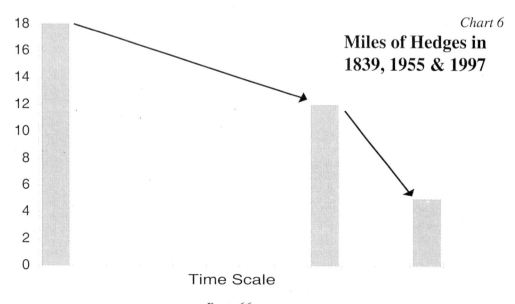

Chart 6
Miles of Hedges in 1839, 1955 & 1997

Time Scale

However, the pace of hedge removal accelerated after 1955 with the rapid growth of the Town Development Scheme. In the 42 years between 1955 and 1997 another 6·8 miles were lost, more than in the previous 116 years. The loss for agricultural purposes was actually less at 2·4 miles, whereas the loss due to development was nearly twice as much at 4·4 miles.

Hedge loss on the Parish Boundary

An additional sample was made involving only the hedges actually on the Parish boundary. Leaving out the "undefined" lengths, and the river banks, in 1839, there were 12·1 miles, by 1997 this was reduced to 7·2 miles, a loss of 4·9 miles or 40%.

This is an annual loss of 0·25% which compares favourably with the loss of 0·45%. of the random sample. The reason for this is the relative distance of the boundary from the developed areas.

Hedge Losses in Other Parishes

Having looked at the figures for hedge removal in Witham, it seemed worthwhile to try a comparison with Bovingdon Hall[1] which is a Countryside Commission Demonstration Farm and with Rivenhall Parish.[2]

The figures for Witham were for a sample and for Bovingdon Hall and Rivenhall Parish were full counts. These figures are shown in Tables 5 and 6.

Table 5 Comparison of Hedge Miles in 3 Parishes

Years of Reference	1803	1839	1945	1955	1977	1997
Bovingdon Hall	79		65		48	
Rivenhall Parish		122			44	
Witham (sample)		18		12		5
Witham (boundary)		12				7

These figures were then combined into 3 periods of 20-30 years to give Table 6

Table 6 Comparison of % Hedge Survival in 3 Parishes

Years of Reference	1803/1839	%	1945/1955	%	1977/1997	%
Bovingdon Hall	79	100	65	82	48	61
Rivenhall	122	100			44	36
Witham (sample)	18	100	12	67	5	28

The figures may be few, but chart 7 shows the comparison of percentages, and the trends are quite clear. Witham and Rivenhall show very similar falls over the period of about 70%, whereas for Bovingdon Hall the decline is much less drastic at 40% loss.

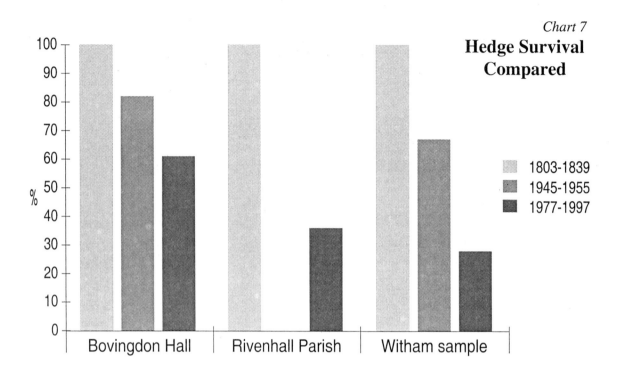

Chart 7
Hedge Survival Compared

Legend:
- 1803-1839
- 1945-1955
- 1977-1997

Size of Fields in Witham

Size	Number of fields	Total in acres
Less than 2 acres	152	
2 - 10	271	1511
10 - 20	95	1260
20 - 50	16	418
meads for hay	7	83
	389	3272

The average (mean) size of field in 1839 was about 8½ acres. My best estimate is that the average size of field in 1997 is about 17 acres. With the variation now between 70 acres on the big farms, and some of the original small fields still in private hands, to talk of an average field has little meaning.

Fortunately, there are still hedges and trees left, but the aerial photographs show how thinly spread they are.

The Effects of Hedge Removal

Hedges are incredibly important for biodiversity, the variety of life, also for farming, landscape, cultural and archaeological reasons. Nationally, hedgerows are important habitats for at least 47 species of conservation concern, including 13 globally threatened or rapidly declining species. This is more than any other habitat. Hedgerows are especially important for butterflies and moths, the smaller farm birds and dormice, while the hedgerow trees are important for the larger birds, bats and invertebrates.

There is growing concern about the rapidly declining numbers of birds which until recently were regarded as common. For example, the skylark which is a ground nesting bird, is believed to have declined by 54% in the years between 1969 and 1992. The song thrush is believed to have declined by a shocking 73% on farmland and 49% in woodland since the mid 1970s.

While neither of these losses are due solely to the loss of hedgerows, it is difficult to separate the removal of hedges from the general intensification of farming methods. There is often increased activity during the nesting season of ground nesting birds, and increased use of autumn sown crops means the loss of the rich feeding on the stubble. There is great pressure to cultivate up to the limits of a field in order to maximise production, and the general tidying up of the countryside means loss of shelter and food for the birds.

The loss of bird life is a symptom of the loss of countless other less visible plants and animals. It is high time that agricultural subsidies were redirected from production only, to sustainable production and conservation of the countryside.

In spite of the loss of 72% of the Witham Parish hedges, I think it is only fair to say that this part of Essex has escaped the worst of the hedge clearances with the consequent "Prairie Look". Other parts of the country and even of Essex are considerably more bare and open. Indeed, there are welcome signs that the tide has turned against hedge removal and there are even some newly planted hedges near Witham.

The traditional method of hedge management in Essex has been by coppicing at regular intervals, cutting down to ground level. This always looks drastic, but can result in thicker hedges with a new lease of life. Many hedges have been neglected and are too thin or straggly to provide any shelter or contribution to the landscape. There is a desperate need for hedges that are wide enough and tall enough and thick enough to be safe havens for wildlife. Together with the headlands and verges, the hedges can provide "Green Corridors" so essential for the survival and movement through the countryside of all types of animals, birds and plants. Again the aerial photos show the thin and sparse nature of some of the hedges.

May I appeal to all who are involved with land management to consider very carefully the contribution hedges make to the landscape and the biodiversity of the countryside. In addition, each one of the surviving hedges is likely to be part of the ancient field system going back for three thousand years, and as such is irreplaceable.

Appendix: Method of sampling the fields for hedge loss

A list was made of all the fields on the Tithe Map in numerical order. Omitted from the sample were the numbers below 351 because there were large gaps and most of the items were too small to be typical fields. Chantrey Wood was too big to be included and the bisecting effect of the "railroad" was ignored.

From this list, I then took the first number i.e. 351 and every subsequent 40th. number. This provided a sample of 13 fields. Then I did this again, starting at numbers 365 and 377 and taking every 40th. number.

Occasionally a number would be missing and then I took the next number. This method has resulted in a sample of 39 fields, about 8% of all the fields on a random basis. It was assumed that all field sides were hedged in 1839. As each field had 4 sides, 2 of which would be shared with adjacent fields, it follows that about 16% of the hedges were sampled. They were measured on the 1874 O.S. 6" map (because it was clear and convenient) and then compared with the 1955 map of Witham and my findings of 1995-7.

1. John Hunter The Age of Hedgerows on a Bocking Estate 1993
2. Rodwell W. A. and K. A. Rivenhall: Investigations of a Villa Church and Village 1993

Coppiced oak tree showing the regrowth from the 'stool' which is about 12 feet in diameter.

Blue Mills, in Witham parish at the time of the Tithe Map. Important crossing point of the River Blackwater. Focal point of ancient field and track systems.

12 The Future

We are now into the 21st. Century, and these reports have all been drawn together, and it becomes apparent to me that this survey of the Witham landscape can only be regarded as the first phase. What started as a simple exercise expanded with the realisation that there are more aspects of the landscape, the hedges and fields that are of great interestand significance and worthy of report.

Consequently, some matters are more fully recorded than others, and as it is several years since I started, it is time for a review anyway. For example, it would be interesting to update and improve the information on:

- the distribution of hops, clematis and woodland thorn

- the girth of all significant trees

- the measurements of coppice stools

- information on ponds e.g. size, shape and distribution especially after the very wet winter of 2000-2001

- the state of the hedges in 2001

- the photographic records

There might well be surprises, not least because there have been hot dry summers and very wet winters. There is a lot more work that could be undertaken in researching other old maps and documents.

It is interesting in the conclusion of this report to quote from a book written nearly 200 years ago and to show that the fascination with hedges and boundaries is not entirely new. My attention has been drawn to a small volume of "The Coverley Papers" from "The Spectator" published in 1710.

In Paper No. 1, Sir Roger de Coverley introduces himself:

I have observed that a Reader seldom peruses a book with pleasure until he knows whether the writer of it be a black or fair man, of mild or choleric disposition, married or a bachelor, with other particulars of the like nature, that conduce very much to the right understanding of an author. To gratify this curiosity which is so natural to a reader ... I must do myself the justice to open the work with my own history.

and then he begins his history:

*I was born to a small hereditary estate, which, according to the tradition of the village where it lies, **was bounded by the same hedges and ditches in William the Conqueror's time that it is at present, and has been delivered down from father to son whole and entire, without the loss or acquisition of a single field or meadow, during the space of six hundred years.***

This is just one extract throwing a fascinating light on the attitude of that particular landowner and the class he represented and the times he lived in and the pride and interest he took in the history of his estate. What changes would he see if he could return now?

What will the landscape of Witham and the surrounding area look like in another two or twenty years, let alone two hundred? In this year of 2001, many changes are taking place. What will the landscape in any part of the country look like? Agriculture and farming methods are under great pressures for change. Farming practices have changed fundamentally in the last 50 years and the effects are visible in the landscape and are demonstrated throughout the environment with the rapid decline in bio-diversity. Will the concerns of the environmentalists be heeded? Can farmers afford to consider the environment unless there are far reaching changes in funding and in the attitudes of governments and politicians?

There will be further development. Only the scale is still uncertain. But if it exceeds the proposals in the Local Plan, then large areas of land may disappear under development. The land surrounding Witham and adjacent to the built-up areas is either graded as high quality agricultural land or designated as Special Landscape Area. Development of this land would therefore mean that not only would good quality cereal land be taken out of production, but the general landscape and the irreplaceable Iron Age landscape could be irrevocably damaged.

I hope that publication of this report, incomplete though it is, will draw attention to and prevent further destruction of this varied, rich and pleasant landscape, probably the oldest, visible part of our heritage, which can so easily be destroyed.

I very much hope that this publication will encourage other and further surveys Every parish is different and unique and fascinating. What is the survival rate for woods, hedges and field systems in your parish? Are there any notable trees, pollarded or otherwise, which may still be marking the bounds after centuries? To make such discoveries for yourself is exciting and recording them could ensure their recognition and improve their chances of survival.

13 Glossary

Measurement of Length

22 yards = 1 Chain
10 chains = 1 Furlong
8 furlongs = 1 Mile
5280 feet = 1 Mile
1760 yards = 1 Mile

Measurement of Area

1 Pole (or Rod or Perch) = 16·5 ft. or 5·5 yds.
1 Pole × 1 Pole = 1 Square Perch (5·5 yds. × 5·5 yds.) = 30·25 sq. yds.
40 Perches = 1 Sq. Rood
4 Sq. Roods = 1 Acre
120 Acres = 1 Hide
640 Acres = 1 Sq. Mile

The Imperial measures were based on very practical everyday pieces of equipment. They probably had local slight variations but would have been recognised as the basis for land use in pre-literate societies.

Chain	The length of the chain which was an integral part of the plough fixings.
Rod, pole or perch	Also part of the plough equipment - for controlling the oxen.
Acre	A day's ploughing for one plough team. Equals one furlong × one chain.
Hide	120 acres. The area of land reckoned to be needed to support one household, but the hide varied in real size according to local conditions and soil, and government demands!

Imperial and Metric Equivalents

1 Acre = 0·4 Hectares
10 Acres = 4·0 Hectares
1 Hectare = 2·47 Acres

Approximate size of the Parish of Witham: 3705 acres = 1482 hectares = 5·78 sq.miles

Length of Parish Boundary = 17·5 miles

14 Bibliography

Addleshaw, G.W.O.	The Development of the Parochial System from Charlemagne (768-814) to Urban 11 1088-1099.
Andrews, D.D., Ed.	Cressing Temple: A Templar & Hospitaller Manor in Essex. 1993.
Aston. Michael, Ed.	The Medieval Landscape of Somerset.
Britnell, R.H.	The Making of Witham. Reprinted from History Studies, University of Durham.
Britnell, R.H.	Agriculture in a Region of Ancient Enclosure 1185-1500. Notts. Medieval Studies Vol. 27 1983.
Clack, David	Spy in the Sky Grant Graphics.
Corke, David	The Nature of Essex. Published by The Essex Naturalists Trust, Barracuda Books Ltd. 1984.
Dartmoor National Park Authority E.C.C.	The Archaeology of Holne Moor Green L.S. Ed. Cressing Conference 1996. The Essex Landscape : In Search of its History.
E.C.C.	Witham. Ivy Chimnies Site, Excavations 1978 Interim report
E.C.C. Planning	Heritage Conservation Group, Witham. Historic Town Project. Assessment Report
E.C.C. Environmental Services Directorate	Essex Biodiversity Action Plan 1999
Gyford, Janet	Domesday Witham.
Gyford, Janet	Witham 1500-1700 Making A Living.
Henderson, Tom	The Parish Church of Saint Nicolas, Witham, Essex. Witham Parochial Church Council, 1986.
Hoskins, W.G.	The Making of the English Landscape.
Hunter, John	The Age of Cressing Field Boundaries. Essex Archaeology and History 28 1997 pp 151-155.
Hunter, John	The Essex Landscape Essex Record Office.
Hunter, John	The Historic Landscape of Cressing Temple & its Environs Cressing Temple. A Templar & Hospitaller Manor in Essex ECC Conference 1993. Ed. David Andrews
Hunter John	The Age of Hedgerows on a Bocking Estate. Essex Archl. Hist. 24
Hunter John	Settlement and Farming Patterns on the mid-Essex Boulder Clays. Essex Archaeol. Hist. 26
Jermyn Stanley T.	Flora of Essex. Essex Naturalists Trust Ltd.1974.
Loyn, H.R.	Anglo-Saxon England and The Norman Conquest Longman 2nd. Edition 1991.
Oosthuizen, Susan	Cambridgeshire from the Air. Alan Sutton. 1991.
MacConnell, J.	Ed. Landscape History and Habitat Management. Symposium Pub. by South Essex Natural History Society 1977.

Muir, Richard and Nina   Fields. MacMillan, London 1989.

Pollard, E., Hooper, M.D.
and Moore, N.W.   Hedges. New Naturalist 1974.

Rackham, Dr. O.   The History of the Countryside. Phoenix, Orion Books Ltd. 1986.

Rackham, Dr. O.   The Illustrated History of the Countryside.
                         Weidenfield and Nicholson, London 1994.

Rodwell, Dr. W.   The Origins and Early Development of Witham, Essex.1993.
                         Oxbow Monographs 1993.

Rodwell, W J and   Rivenhall: Investigations of a Villa, Church and Village,
     Rodwell, K.A.   1950-1977. Vols. 1 and 2, Council for British Archaeology 1993

Scarfe, Norman   A Shell Guide Essex. Faber and Faber. 1975.

Strachan, David   Essex From the Air. Essex County Council 1988.

Tiller, Kate   English Local History An Introduction, Alan Sutton 1992.

Williamson, Tom   Parish Boundaries, Early Fields, Continuity and Discontinuity.
                         Journal of Historical Geography. **12,** 3 (1986).

Winchester, Angus   Discovering Parish Boundaries   Shire Publications, 1990.
Institute of Geological
Sciences 1972   Sand and Gravel Resources of the Country around Witham.

Documents

"The Spectator"   No. 1 Thursday March 1st. 1710-11, Coverley Papers.
Chapman and Andre   Map of Essex, 1777.
Ordnance Survey Maps,
6" Edition 1874-5.   Various 1900-1999.

E.R.O. D/CT 405   The Tithe Map Survey   Witham
E.R.O. D/CT 49   "   Little Braxted
E.R.O. D/CT 109   "   Cressing
E.R.O. D/CT 136   "   Faulkbourne
E.R.O. D/CT 137   "   Fairstead
E.R.O. D/CT 167   "   Hatfield Peverel
E.R.O. D/CT 290   "   Rivenhall
E.R.O. D/CT 344   "   Terling
E.R.O. D/CT 396   "   Wickham Bishops
E.R.O. D/Du 850   The Bounds of the Parish of Witham 1815.

Bulletins of The Witham and Countryside Society.

White's Directory for Essex, 1848.